Pearson
PUBLISHING

Student Handbook
Applications of ICT

for KS3, KS4 and GCSE

Gareth Williams

Illustrations by Nic Brennan

Name..

Address ....

....

....

Dates of exam: ....

Coursework deadline dates: ....

....

Exam board..

Syllabus number...

Candidate number ....

Centre number...

Further copies of this publication may be obtained from:

Pearson Publishing
Chesterton Mill, French's Road, Cambridge CB4 3NP
Tel 01223 350555   Fax 01223 356484

Email info@pearson.co.uk   Web site http://www.pearsonpublishing.co.uk/

ISBN: 1 85749 577 2

Published by Pearson Publishing 2001
© Pearson Publishing 2001

First reprint 2001

Contents

Information and Communication Technology (ICT) is used in every aspect of our lives. If someone 20 years ago had described the way we currently use computers, mobile phones and the Internet it would have been called science fiction. Sometimes when students are asked, "Where are computers used outside the home and school?" there is some hesitation. However, had the question been "Where are computers **not** used outside the home and school?", the answer would have been more difficult to find.

The shops where we buy clothes and food use computers to scan items at the checkout till. Some toys have computers embedded in them, while the cars in which we drive to school were built and painted by computerised robots. Mountaineers use satellite links to keep in touch with their families, while we can all keep in touch with our families and friends around the world by email. The Meteorological Office uses a supercomputer to run a computer model to forecast the weather, while the police can identify criminals from a computer database of DNA records.

Information on almost every subject is available from the Internet where powerful search engines can locate articles in less than a second from the billions of pages available. Purchasing food and clothes online means we can choose to shop from home, while mobile phones allow us to be contacted at all times.

This handbook describes how some of the larger organisations in the UK use ICT. Many have been involved with computers for 30 to 40 years, since the time when computers were operated by valves and occupied vast air-conditioned rooms. Although much has changed since those early days, there still seems no end to the continuing development of new technology and so this book is just a snapshot of some of the systems and procedures currently in use.

This book provides an insight into the way ICT is used in a small but important group of businesses and organisations that affect our daily lives. In your study of ICT, whether at Key Stage 3 or 4, GCSE or A-level, the knowledge of these applications is a necessary part of the syllabus. The book can be used in conjunction with the *Student Handbook for ICT*.

Using this book

If this is your own book, you may decide to personalise it. Use the margin to make notes and the space provided in the questions to pencil in your answers before checking them with those given at the back of the book (see pages 112 to 115). The contents page has been designed in the form of a checklist so that you can monitor and assess your progress as you work through the book. The index at the back of the book will help you to find specific topics.

Feedback

If you have any comments or suggestions as to how this book may be improved or updated, please send them to the author via Pearson Publishing.

When it comes to using a computer, the software – the programs running on the computer – are just as important as the hardware; without software the computer would be unusable. Software for use in homes and schools is purchased 'off-the-shelf' in standard, self-contained packages that can be installed easily onto computers. Examples include software for word processing, databases, spreadsheets, games, learning and revision.

Some of the standard software mentioned above is vital for business and industry. For example, businesses use word processing software for writing letters to customers and clients and spreadsheets are used for forecasting sales. In larger organisations, specialist software may be needed to operate the business. For example, supermarkets will need software to work with bar code readers and produce itemised till receipts for customers at the checkout.

When specialist software is required by an organisation, programs can either be written by programmers within the organisation or by a specialist company. The advantages and disadvantages relating to each of these ways are outlined later in this section (see page 8). Firstly, we will look at how standard 'off-the-shelf' software packages are used commercially.

Word processors

In businesses and organisations around the world, the word processor is a standard office tool. In the past, letters, reports, notices, instruction leaflets and books were all produced on mechanical typewriters. Now, word processing software allows work to be edited onscreen by inserting and deleting words, moving words, sentences and paragraphs around and checking the spelling before printing.

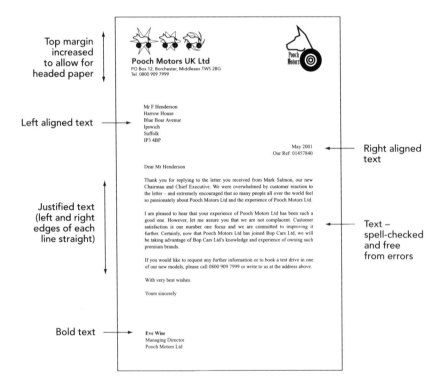

A business letter written on a word processor

Microsoft® Word is the most commonly used word processing software. It is used in many countries around the world. The QWERTY keyboard is also standard in many countries even though the original layout of the keys, designed more than a 100 years ago, was intended to separate the commonly used keys to avoid the hammers on the typewriters from jamming. The keyboard layout varies slightly between countries to provide the different characters used in their alphabets.

Desktop publishing (DTP)

In the past, when businesses needed to produce materials such as brochures and advertisements, they used specialist design companies. Now, with powerful personal computers and sophisticated desktop publishing packages, many organisations produce their own materials in-house. Desktop publishing programs allow users to look at the page of a document as a whole and design the layout by marking areas for text and graphics. They can be used to produce posters, brochures, advertisements, letter-headed paper, compliment slips, menus, catalogues, price lists, signs, etc.

Borders

Inserted graphics

Different font styles and sizes

This advertisement illustrates several of the features of a desktop publishing package

Spreadsheets

Spreadsheet programs can be found in most businesses and organisations where numbers are used. The program is designed to display and process numbers. It is made up of a grid into which numbers are entered. The program contains many mathematical, statistical and financial operations that can be applied to the numbers in a fraction of a second. Before the age of computers, these tasks had to be done by hand which took a long time and were prone to error. The software can also produce graphs and charts.

Spreadsheets have many uses, eg for analysing sales figures, planning and making budgets, creating company accounts and mathematical modelling. The illustration on the following page shows a spreadsheet being used to analyse the vehicle costs in a transport company.

	A	B	C	D	E
1					
2	Vehicle registration	P727WTN			
3		Distance	Fuel used	Repairs	
4		(Kilometres)	(Litres)	Costs	
5	Jan	3465	600		
6	Feb	3006	535	£410.98	
7	Mar	4117	720		
8	Apr	3344	590	£230.30	
9	May	3667	620		
10	Jun	4022	715		
11	Jul	3766	640		
12	Aug	4666	815		
13	Sep	4218	722		
14	Oct	1866	325	£1022.20	
15	Nov	3043	545		
16	Dec	3682	644		
17					
18	Total	42862	7471	£1663.48	
19	Average number of kilometres per litre=		5.7		
20	Average cost of fuel (per litre)=		£0.79		
21	Annual fuel costs=		£5902.09		
22					
23	Total costs including repairs		£7565.57		
24					
25					
26					
27					

Annotations:
- =SUM(D5:D16) — Formula to add up the numbers in the column
- =SUM(B5:B16)
- =SUM(C5:C16)
- =B18/C18 — Calculate the kpl by dividing the kilometres travelled by the litres used
- =C18*C20 — Litres used multiplied by cost of each litre
- =C21+D18 — Fuel + repair costs

A spreadsheet to analyse the annual cost of running a lorry. If a 'distance' or 'fuel used' value needs to be corrected, the revised calculations are performed in a fraction of a second

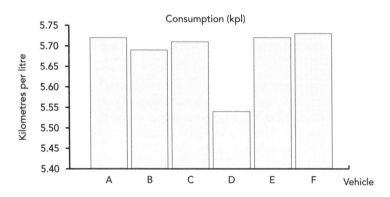

By comparing fuel consumption graphs for different lorries, it becomes clear very quickly that vehicle D's engine is not running efficiently

Databases

A database is a collection of related data items, which are linked and structured so that the data can be accessed in a number of ways. Databases are very useful to organisations of all sizes as up-to-date information can be held in a database. The information might be about customers or to do with the goods held in stock. It might be the patient records in a hospital or the bookings made for a theatre or airline. Whatever the need, a database can ensure the operation of a business runs smoothly by storing, sorting, retrieving, displaying and printing the information.

Although standard database programs like Microsoft® Access can be purchased as part of the Microsoft® Office family of programs, it requires a reasonable knowledge and expertise by the user to create a working database. With the construction of larger databases that need to be accessed by more than one user at the same time (multi-user databases), experienced computer programmers are required to set up the system.

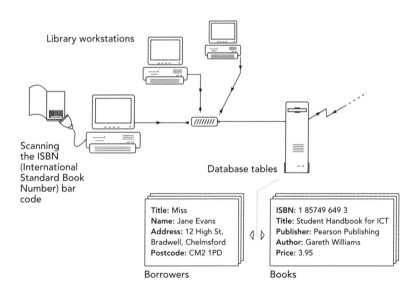

A library database system – Connections over a wide area network to other libraries. The scanned ISBN number is passed to the database where a search is carried out. Links between different database tables allow book details to be linked to the borrower

Presentation packages

A presentation is when someone gives a talk to a group of people on a particular topic. Visual aids can help to make a presentation more interesting. The presentation software package allows a presenter to prepare their talk as a set of slides using text and graphics. The user can animate the screen displays by making the text and graphics move around the screen in different ways. Sound effects can also be added. In business, presentations are made to put across ideas and knowledge or to sell products and services.

A popular presentation package is PowerPoint, which is part of the Microsoft® Office set of programs. Users are given a choice with this package of starting the presentation from a blank set of slides or using one of the 'wizard' or ready-made slide sets. These structured slide sets, which cover most of the common types of business presentations, include:

- Business training
- The marketing plan
- Presenting business plans
- How to sell products and services
- Presentations to company meetings
- How to motivate staff

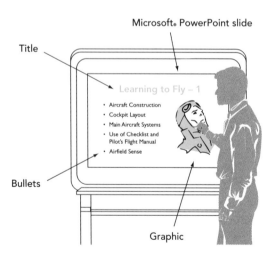

The computer display can be projected onto a screen when presenting to larger groups

Specialist software needs to be written when standard programs are not available to carry out the required task. For example, it would be unlikely that your local computer store would stock a package to store the 46 million fingerprint images held on the Police National Computer and be able to compare these at the rate of a million a second! For applications of this nature, computer programmers must write the software specifically for the organisation.

'Do you have Fingerprint version 2.0?!'

There is also increasing pressure on businesses to make use of the Internet. To begin with this might involve creating Web pages to advertise the company and its products. The next stage might be to sell over the Internet, which means taking credit card payments from customers, and ensuring credit card numbers are secure by encrypting the data. Following this would be to link customer orders to despatching goods, stock control and reordering products. An integrated system of this nature would help many businesses to run more efficiently and reduce their costs. The software systems required for these tasks need to be tailored by programmers for the business.

When an organisation requires specialist software to be written, the software can be:

- written in-house
- outsourced (written for the organisation by another company).

Software written in-house

Many businesses have IT departments and employ staff to look after the computers, run networks and write computer software. When new software applications need to be written, the task is passed to the computer programmers within the company.

Some of the advantages and disadvantages of writing software in-house are summarised below:

Advantages

- In-house programmers have a better understanding of how the business operates.

- Meetings to discuss the requirements and progress of the new software are easy to arrange.

Disadvantages

- Employing additional computer programmers is expensive for the company.

- Staff within the company may not have the necessary knowledge and experience for new projects.

Outsourcing

Outsourcing is when an organisation makes a contract with a computer software company for them to develop and support the IT requirements of the organisation. Outsourcing to specialist computer companies is not unusual in medium and larger businesses.

There are two forms of outsourcing. One is where the software is purchased and so the organisation that has paid for the work to be done owns it. The second form of outsourcing is where the software is rented from the computer software company. The companies that provide rented software are called application service providers (ASPs) and these companies are detailed on pages 9 and 10.

When an organisation decides to outsource their IT work it is essential that they provide a very precise specification of the work needed. If this is not done, it is quite possible that the software supplied by the outsourcing company will not provide the solution required. The contract between the two companies should be a legal agreement and must include the deadline for completion and any penalties that will be imposed if the software performs poorly or is delivered late. Although great care must be taken when setting up an agreement, there are several advantages for an organisation to outsource the work. Take, for example, some of the new projects being implemented by the police force. By outsourcing IT work, the police can concentrate on their 'core business', which is keeping law and order. The specialist computer company can provide a greater number of programmers with a wider experience of the latest methods. Often, when an outsourcing contract is made, IT staff move across to work in the outsourcing company. This move helps both the project and the careers of the staff involved as they gain more experience with the IT company.

Two examples of major outsourcing contracts:

- The UK Government Inland Revenue department formed a contract with Electronic Data Systems, a Texas-based company, in 1994 to produce a new system for collecting taxes.

- The Police Force awarded the contract for the National Automated Fingerprint Identification System (NAFIS) to the American company, TWS, in 1995. This outsourced project, worth £96m, had a detailed specification in paper form that was one metre thick.

Application service providers (ASPs)

When a business needs specialist software and services, rather than buy them from an outside company, they can rent them instead. Computer companies that rent software are called application service providers (ASPs). For example, a company may need to integrate ICT into everyday business by installing automated ordering systems through their Internet Web site. If the company were unable to develop such a system in-house, they could rent the software from an ASP.

The most common software supplied by ASPs includes supporting the management with stock lists, products costs, purchasing stock and sales. When a business uses this software they become more competitive, can provide a better customer service and they can reduce waste by better purchasing decisions. Another major advantage of renting software is that there is a fixed fee per user each month. This is much easier to budget for than a large initial payment when software is purchased and then the ongoing support costs for running the software.

Once an agreement has been made with an ASP, the software and all the data is held on the ASP's server. This means that the business using the software only needs an Internet browser on their workstation or a thin client computer (a very basic computer with a small hard drive and few installed software programs).

Working with the software over the Internet can produce its own problems. The speed, reliability and security of access are all issues that the business would need to address. For critical applications, private or leased communication lines might be necessary.

Many people have email accounts on the Internet with Hotmail. This is an example of an ASP software application provided by Microsoft although they do not charge for its use.

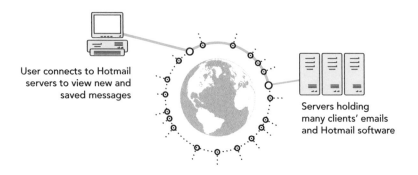

User connects to Hotmail servers to view new and saved messages

Servers holding many clients' emails and Hotmail software

Hotmail – An example of free application service provider software

Questions

1 A holiday hotel in Antigua specialising in water sports uses software on their computer network that keeps track of how much hotel guests are spending. Computer workstations, located in the beach restaurant, the hotel bar, the gift shop and the reception are connected together by a local area network (LAN).

When guests visit the restaurant or make purchases at the bar and shop, they sign for the goods and give their room number. The cost of the meals and goods are stored on the computer and when the guest comes to settle their account, a list of purchases and the total bill are printed at the workstation in reception.

a The hotel only uses Windows 98 and the Microsoft® Office applications on their network consisting of Word (word processor), Excel (spreadsheet) and Access (database). Which of these three programs would be the best to use to perform the task outlined above? Justify your choice.

....

....

....

....

b List three other tasks that the computer could be used for in the running of the holiday hotel.

i ....

....

ii ....

....

iii..

....

2 The head of ICT in a school was asked to prepare a talk to give to a group of parents about a new A-level course. As the room they are using has a computer workstation and projection unit, what would be the best software package to use to assist with the talk?

....

3 Complete the following sentences by choosing the correct words from the list below:

   software   Hotmail   outsourcing   ASP   rented

.... is when an organisation makes a contract with a computer software company to provide its software and support requirements. This .... can either be purchased or .... If the software is rented, it is obtained from an (application service provider) ....

................................, an Internet email service, is an example of software from an ASP although there is no charge for its use.

4 Link items in the three lists by drawing lines across the page. Match the left column of software package types with the middle column of Microsoft® software names with the right column listing a type of task to be done. For example, a word processor links to Microsoft® Word which links to writing a letter:

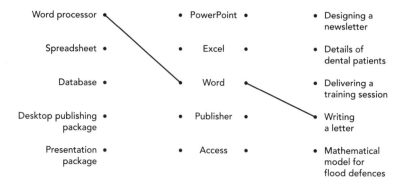

When considering the applications of Information and Communication Technology (ICT), one of the most important developments is that of the Internet. The Internet has changed the way in which we communicate with people, the way we buy and sell goods and services, and how we can obtain information.

It was only recently that the Internet celebrated its 30th birthday. It was started in 1969 as a research project funded by the US military. By the end of that year, a total of four computers were linked to the network. Today, millions of users are connected and communicating with each other across a global network.

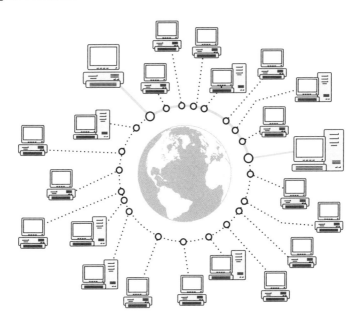

The Internet now has millions of users who access it daily

Some Web sites receive more visits (hits) than others. The official Web site for the 2000 Olympic Games received six and a half billion hits over a ten-day period while the games were in progress. This represents an average of 7500 hits per second, 24 hours a day.

The development of the Internet continues at an ever increasing pace. Connecting to the Internet by dialling up via a modem from a computer may soon be a thing of the past. 'Always on' connections will replace the need to dial up. Access to the Internet will be available through a range of household appliances such as TVs, microwaves and fridges as well as mobile phones and in cars. Speech recognition software is developing to the stage where voice input can replace keyboard entry and major work is underway to install cabling across the country to speed up the flow of data between cities and towns.

e-business

e-business, also known as e-commerce, is the name given to trading over the Internet. This might be between one business and another, for example a manufacturer ordering materials, and is called B2B (business to business). Or it might involve using the Internet to sell to consumers, called B2C (business to consumer). Business on the Internet is rapidly changing the way in which we buy and sell goods and online trading is forecast to reach a trillion (1000 billion) pounds worldwide by 2003.

Selling goods over the Internet opens up new markets. Internet Web sites are accessible around the world and so all companies, both large and small, have equal opportunities to reach new international markets 24 hours a day, 365 days of the year. One investment company in the United States took 20 years to accumulate $100 bn of customer investments. With the aid of

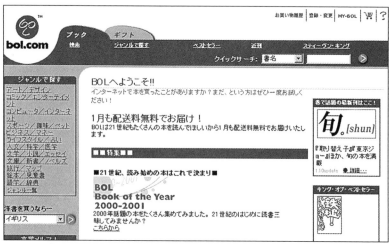

Some international sites allow users to select the language they want

the Internet, they were able to take the next $100 bn within six months. Making the Web site effective for selling on an international scale requires careful planning. For example, one Internet bookshop site offers users a choice of Web pages in 13 different languages.

The amount of use a company will make of the Internet depends on the type of business, the commitment of senior managers and the ability and expertise of the staff to design and implement the new systems. The use that is made of the Internet in business can be divided into different levels:

Level 1   Using email to send messages or letters to other staff in the company or to customers and suppliers. Large datafiles can also be attached to the emails and sent around the world in a matter of seconds.

Level 2   Businesses can create Web sites where customers can view the products and read detailed descriptions of both the goods and the company. Customers can also contact the company by email via the Web site.

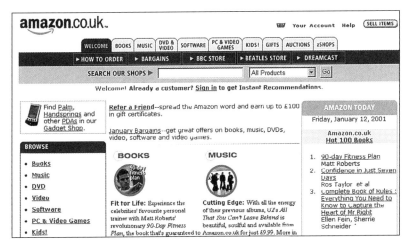

Level 3   Customers can place their orders via the Web site and pay for the goods by credit cards over a secure (encrypted) link. Customers may be able to view whether the goods are in stock and track the progress of their order. The business may offer service and support over the Internet to the customer.

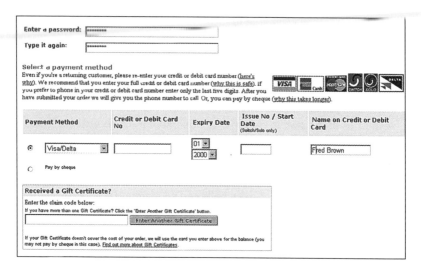

Level 4   Orders placed by customers over the Internet start automated processes in the business. These might include ordering parts from suppliers, scheduling the time and date for making the goods, and reserving space on the delivery lorry. The customer's payment is also fully integrated into the company's account systems.

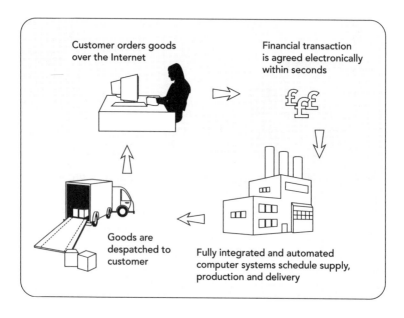

Customer orders goods over the Internet

Financial transaction is agreed electronically within seconds

Goods are despatched to customer

Fully integrated and automated computer systems schedule supply, production and delivery

Typical stages involved in buying goods over the Internet are as follows:

- **Locating the company's Web site** – This can be found by either using an Internet search engine or by typing in the site address, eg www.tescodirect.com. Once the site has been found, it can be saved as a favourite.

- **Browsing the products on the site** – Most sites use menus to group the products making it easier for specific goods to be found. Often detailed information is given and some companies, for example online bookshops, encourage users to write reviews of products that are then available for other customers to read. Where browsing for products takes a while to do, for example when doing an Internet supermarket shop, details of the goods are downloaded onto the hard drive of the computer. This enables the browsing to be done off-line without running up large telephone bills. Sophisticated Web site software can allow users to design their goods by choosing from a range of styles, colours and options. The software then displays the finished product and price according to the choices made.

- **Placing an order** – While browsing the site, the selected items are stored in a 'virtual' basket or trolley. Payment details are then entered. These include indicating the type of credit card (MasterCard, Visa, Switch, American Express or a store card), the card number and its expiry date. Before these details are transmitted back across the Internet, the data is encrypted (put in code) for security. Other information may also be requested depending on the goods being ordered, for example, for a fresh food order a delivery time is selected.

- **Checking the progress of the order** – Many companies provide feedback on the progress of the order. This can be via the Web site on the Internet or by email. For example, an email is often generated automatically to confirm the order and give estimated delivery dates, and further emails are generated once the goods are dispatched.

Web site design

For businesses selling goods over the Internet it is very important to have a well-designed Web site. Some of the largest retail stores failed to sell goods over the Internet when they first designed Web pages because customers were leaving the site before a purchase had been made. The reasons for this included frustrating delays while complex graphics were downloaded, poorly-designed navigation tools that made it difficult for customers to find the goods they were looking for and complicated ordering procedures.

A well-designed Web site should include the following features:

- Web pages appear quickly (without delays as graphic images are loaded)
- the page design fits the user's screen
- the pages look professional and do not have spelling or grammatical errors
- the site can be navigated easily and products located quickly
- a search facility where goods can be located using only part of the description
- instructions for first-time users
- out-of-stock products are marked
- pictures and brief descriptions and reviews of the goods are shown
- ordering of goods is straightforward
- payment of goods is done using secure encryption techniques.

Because Web sites can be accessed from around the world, a further consideration is to offer a choice of languages to the user.

The illustration on page 19 shows some of the pages you might find on a typical business Web site selling goods to consumers.

Web site design

Some typical pages included in
B2C (business to customer) Web sites

 Home page. This is the first page users see. It should be
attractive and will contain links to the other pages.

 Once the customer has selected some goods, this page
allows order details to be entered, often credit card details.
Data from this page is usually encrypted for security.

 Help is available to aid the customer to use and
purchase goods from the site.

 This/these page(s) show the products for sale. Often
there may be descriptions and pictures of the products.

 Some sites use a virtual trolley in which users can place
goods they wish to purchase as they browse the products.

 Most sites include a 'contact us' page allowing users to email
or telephone the company if they have specific questions.

The way the Web site integrates with the office computers is very important
for the business. When a customer places an order with a site on the
Internet, an efficient office computer system will ensure the process of
completing the order is carried out smoothly and in such a way that the
customer will be happy to return to the site in the future to order more
goods. For the majority of businesses, their Web site is linked to database
programs that hold product details and the level of stock.

Some of the processes that occur in businesses after an order is placed are outlined below:

- recording details of the customer and their purchase on computer file
- processing the credit card details and electronically transferring the money from the customers account to the business
- generating instructions for goods to be picked, packaged and despatched from the warehouse
- reducing the number of items in stock on the computer database and ordering more goods if the number in stock has reached the minimum level
- automatically emailing the customer with confirmation of the order and delivery dates.

Electronic mail

Almost all people with an Internet connection regularly send and receive emails. In business it is a vital means of communication between staff and with outside companies. In a survey of staff in large companies, more than half of those questioned said that receiving an email message boosted their day while no email made some staff irritable.

As well as sending and receiving text messages, email software enables files to be attached with the message. The attached files could be word processor documents being passed around for editing or spreadsheet files to illustrate the sales figures. Electronic mail has transformed the way we operate. Whether we need to send files, documents, graphic images or customer information, email can pass these around the world in seconds.

In recent years there have been a number of cases where companies have been embarrassed in public or have been taken to court because their staff have included rude or libellous (false statements that might damage another's reputation) remarks in their emails. Some companies have introduced 'Email policies' for staff insisting that email content is always polite and courteous and banning all racist and obscene comments and any mention of competitors and rival organisations.

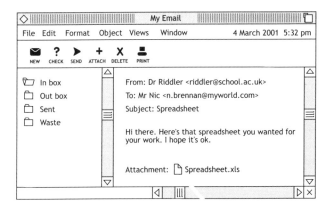

	A	B	C
1	Sample	Growth(%)	Feed(mg)
2	B13400067	10.2	3
3	B13400068	13.4	6
4	B13400069	17.4	9
5	B13400070	6.7	12

Files can also be attached to email text messages

Spam

Spam is the name given to unsolicited emails that are sent out in huge quantities – sometimes in millions at a time – to users on the Internet. Unsolicited mail is mail that has not been requested by the user. The majority of this unwanted email is trying to sell products and services but it also includes 'get-rich-quick' schemes, chain letters, health cures, loan and credit schemes and pornography. Spam costs businesses a great deal of money. Companies try to filter the spam mail out before it reaches staff but this is seldom completely successful. Once the email reaches staff then useful work time is lost while staff sort out the 'real' business emails from the unsolicited ones. Spam emails can also clog up the network blocking normal business taking place. An independent report released in 1998 revealed that spam cost UK business £5 bn per year.

Making telephone calls over the Internet

The big attraction of making phone calls over the Internet for both business and home users is the cost saving. To connect to the Internet is the cost of a local call. If long distance or international phone calls are then made over the Internet there are considerable cost savings. Many traditional phone companies are already saving money by routing international calls over the Internet although this is seldom mentioned to customers!

The proper name for this form of communication is voice over IP (VoIP), where IP stands for Internet protocol. Users need a sound card in their computer and a microphone and speakers. Headset units with microphones are popular for frequent use as it leaves the hands free for using the keyboard. Calls can be made to other users with computers that are set up with the VoIP software installed or calls can be directed to normal telephones where the signal leaves the Internet a few miles before the final connection to join the normal telephone system. The speech quality is similar to making a call from a mobile phone and users receiving the call on normal phones would be unaware that the call was being made over the Internet. VoIP is slowly becoming more popular with companies as new cable structures provide greater bandwidth for Internet traffic.

Disadvantages of the Internet

Internet abuse

With so many computers in business now connected to the Internet, employers are finding that workers are using the Internet for personal use during their working hours. This use includes sending personal emails, using chat lines and browsing the network for personal interest. People also download music MP3 files, access pornographic material and even do their shopping! It has been reported that as much as a third of employee time in some companies is spent accessing the Web for personal use. This represents a considerable loss to the company, not only because the employee is not doing productive work for the company during this time but is also using valuable computer resources.

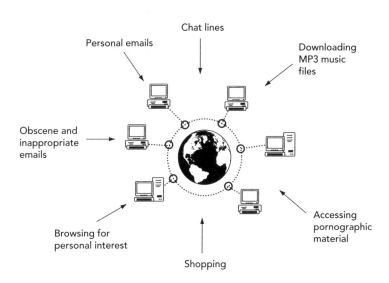

Chat lines

Personal emails

Downloading MP3 music files

Obscene and inappropriate emails

Browsing for personal interest

Shopping

Accessing pornographic material

Abuse of the Internet in business

Companies have different attitudes to using the Internet for personal use. Some companies encourage employees to surf the Net so that they have a broader knowledge of events and claim that from this, employees have introduced new ideas into the business. Other companies ignore personal use of the Internet and only judge the effectiveness of their employees by the amount they achieve, while other companies prohibit personal use altogether and monitor their workers' emails and the sites they visit on the Internet.

More companies are now insisting that workers sign a code of conduct for Internet use. This code makes it an offence to forward words or pictures that are 'offensive, harassing, obscene, racist, sexist, threatening or libellous'. A number of companies have dismissed staff for 'inappropriate' use of the Internet and email. A mobile phone company dismissed 40 staff for sending obscene emails and a chemical company has dismissed and disciplined up to 300 staff for similar offences. The IT department in one company ran their own profit-making travel agency from the Internet and in another organisation a person created a 20,000 user site for MP3 music files on the company's server.

With so much business now being done using computers and the Internet, any disruption to either can cause major problems for companies. Computer viruses are designed specifically to cause this disruption and when they are released through the Internet they spread very rapidly. Viruses are small programs that find their way onto the hard disks of computers and can destroy the data stored there. Viruses also make copies of themselves to infect other computers, either by hitching a lift on a floppy disk or by travelling across the network.

Many different forms of virus have been written. Some will destroy all the data on the hard disk of a computer, which could be very serious if this hard disk was in a company's network file server. In fact, this type of virus is not as damaging as some. Most companies keep backup tapes that can be used to restore important data. Much more serious are viruses that make small changes to the data in files on the disk. These can often be destroying data for weeks or months before they are detected by which time restoring from backup tapes is very much more difficult. By the autumn of 2000 there were 56,000 different known PC viruses.

In May 2000, a computer student in the Philippines launched one of the most damaging viruses to date onto the Internet. Named the 'Love Bug', this virus appeared as an email with 'I love you' as the subject. The email contained an attached file that, when opened, automatically forwarded the virus to every user listed in that person's email address book. Within hours of the virus being released, businesses around the world were grinding to a halt under the sheer volume of email traffic. The virus also corrupted files in the computer. From a survey taken after the virus attack the estimated cost to businesses worldwide was ten billion dollars.

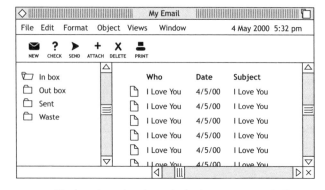

The love bug virus brought business to a standstill

In the summer of 2000, the first virus appeared on mobile phone software. With the move towards 'always connected' third generation mobile phones (see page 27), it is likely that the problem of viruses will continue to grow in this area too.

Hackers

A report by an IT research group in the autumn of 2000 stated that half of the small and medium-sized companies in the UK would suffer an attack from hackers by 2003. With most businesses connected to the Internet, hackers are able to gain access to the computers through the network. Small and medium-sized companies are more likely to be targeted because they seldom have the sophisticated security systems used by large organisations.

Hackers are people who gain unauthorised access to other people's computer systems, programs and data. In order to do this, hackers must have a very good knowledge of computer operating systems (eg Unix and Windows NT) and use programs tools for monitoring, scanning ports and cracking passwords.

There are two types of hackers, those that cause damage and those who call themselves 'ethical' hackers. The worst types of hacker are those that break into computer systems to cause damage to the company by changing or stealing data. Even if a company's Web page is altered 'for a joke' the impact can be serious because consumers, seeing that the site is not secure, may lose confidence and stop purchasing online using credit cards. 'Ethical' hackers do not change or destroy data. Their objective is to expose weaknesses in the security systems that companies use. For example, although an early operating system had very little security built in, it was being promoted for use with online purchasing and banking. Hackers were able to expose the weaknesses and force the manufacture to improve the security of the software. These 'ethical' hackers are increasingly being consulted, and even employed, by government and software security organisations for their knowledge and expertise.

One form of Internet hacking is called a 'Denial of service' attack. One or more hackers will generate a flood of random requests directed at an Internet company. This huge amount of data will block the lines for normal business and the company will be unable to trade until the attack is stopped. These attacks have been directed at major international companies with the result that millions of pounds have been wiped off their shares prices as confidence in the companies has fallen. 'Denial of service' attacks may become more common as home users are linked to faster Internet connections like ADSL and broadband with larger bandwidths.

Although mobile phones have been around for a number of years, the first wireless application protocol or WAP phones were only launched in the UK in 1999. A WAP mobile phone can access the Internet as well as make ordinary phone calls. 'Wireless application protocol' means that the digital signals sent to and from the mobile conform to standards agreed by the different phone manufacturers.

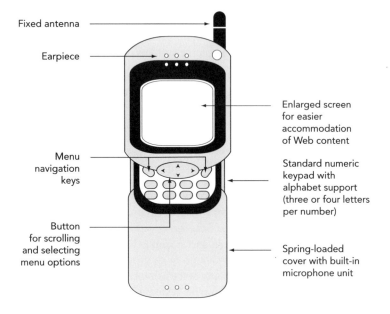

Fixed antenna

Earpiece

Enlarged screen for easier accommodation of Web content

Menu navigation keys

Standard numeric keypad with alphabet support (three or four letters per number)

Button for scrolling and selecting menu options

Spring-loaded cover with built-in microphone unit

Although WAP phones can access the Internet, they do not receive the colour Internet pages with graphics and pictures as displayed on desktop computers. The Web pages designed for mobile phones are text only and designed for the small screens. Existing Web pages written in HTML need to be rewritten in wireless mark-up language (WML).

The current WAP phones have small monochrome screens (usually green and black) and the data transfer speed is quite slow. The technology to improve and develop the mobile phones over the next few years is generally known and these developments are currently underway.

It has been common practice in ICT to group products into 'generations' according to their technological advancement. For example, the first computers were made with electronic valves similar in size to small light bulbs. These became known as first generation computers. When the transistor was developed they replaced the glass valves making the computers much smaller, faster and requiring less power. These became known as second generation computers. Integrated circuits then replaced transistors and these computers became the third generation. The same process of grouping products into 'generations' has been applied to mobile phones:

- **1G** – The first mobile phones using analogue signals (a signal wave constantly varying according to the frequency and volume of the speech). These were only suitable for voice transmissions, not data.

- **2G** – 1999. WAP phones capable of connecting to the Internet and sending short text messages. It uses Global System for Mobile Communications (GSM), which delivers a speed of 9.6 kbps (kilo bits per second). This is slow in comparison with home computer connections with modems of 56 kbps.

- **2.5G** – Forecast for 2001. This is an interim stage before the third generation, hence the half generation. These mobiles will use General Packet Radio Service (GPRS), which have much faster data rates of 115 kbps. With this system, users are always connected to the Internet, there is no need to dial for a connection.

- **3G** – Forecast for 2002 but some experts predict 2003 to 2005 is more likely. These mobile units will use a system called Universal Mobile Telecommunications System (UMTS), which will transmit up to 2 Mbps of data. At these speeds mobiles will even be able to receive full colour TV and video.

In April 2000, the government auctioned the licences that would enable the telecommunication companies to operate 3G (third generation) mobile communications. They restricted the number of licences to five and raised £22.5 billion in the sale, enough money to buy 180 new hospitals! This was a lot more money than the government had expected to raise. Because the companies had to pay so much for the licences, the users of these new mobile devices will have to pay more for the services provided.

With the introduction of WAP mobile phones a new word, m-commerce, has become popular. The 'm', standing for mobile, and commerce, another word for trading, means buying, selling and other business services from a mobile connected to the Internet. Current applications allow the user to:

- view bank balances, pay bills, view recent transactions and transfer money between accounts
- obtain the latest share prices
- check train times, current delays and cancellations
- order and pay for foreign currency
- make airline reservations and purchase tickets
- view the latest news headlines and receive weather forecasts
- view the latest sports news, eg football results
- view the latest travel news to avoid traffic jams
- make restaurant bookings.

Some examples of applications are as follows:

- A hotel chain with 56 hotels across the country has launched a WAP service that allows customers to check from their mobile phones if a room is available at one the hotels, to make a reservation and to receive travel directions.

- Coinless vending machines are being installed where mobile phone customers can purchase food and drinks by calling the machine's unique number direct from their mobile. The cost of purchases appear on the customer's phone account.

- A high street travel agent has provided online access with the WAP browser to holiday information. Details of special offers, flights, city guides and weather reports are all available to customers through their WAP mobile phone.

- One of the UK's largest supermarket chains has launched a WAP mobile phone ordering service. The service is targeted at customers looking for last minute purchases of flowers, champagne and chocolates. They also give news of special offers and include a daily recipe for mobile customers.

The technology and applications of mobile Internet phones are still in their infancy. Users are upgrading their slower WAP phones to the new GPRS WAP systems with high data speeds and the 'always on' link to the Internet.

An interesting feature of mobile phones that are constantly connected to the Internet is that the location of the phone can be calculated. This means that businesses can send messages to customers on their phones advertising special offers on goods in shops where the user is just passing by or offering a discount coupon for a meal in a restaurant close by. If customers need cash then the phone will provide directions to the nearest cash dispenser (ATM). Soon customers will be able to order fast food as they approach the restaurant and pay for goods, food, taxis and buses all from their mobile phone without the need for credit cards and cash.

1 Complete the following sentences by choosing the correct words from the list below:

*search   quickly   customer   spelling   home
encryption   language*

Well-designed Web pages should appear ……………….. and not contain ……………….. and grammatical errors. To help the user find products, Web sites use ……………….. facilities. When making payments for goods on the Internet, the Web site should use secure ……………….. techniques.

2 List three different features of a Web site that might stop a customer from placing an order to purchase goods from the site or from returning to the site to place future orders.

a ....

b ....

c ....

3 Links are used to move between different pages on Web sites. These links are illustrated in the diagram below by arrows, an arrow at both ends of the line indicates that the user can move backwards and forwards but a single arrow shows movement in one direction only.

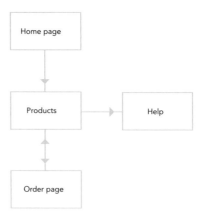

Several important links are missing in the design of the Web pages. Mark on the diagram the missing links and explain why they are needed.

....

....

....

....

....

....

....

4 What do the following Internet abbreviations stand for?

a B2B ....

b B2C ....

5 A small British company manufactures model electric trains and then sells them to toy shops in London. If they decided to use their Web site to advertise and sell the models worldwide, list two changes that they might need to make to their Web site or the business.

a ....

b ....

6 Give two reasons why spam email is a nuisance for business.

a ....

....

b ....

....

7 State two differences between a 2G (second generation) and a 3G (third generation) mobile phone.

a ....

....

b ....

....

3 ICT in supermarkets

Computers are vital to the operation of a supermarket store. If you have ever experienced the situation of being in a supermarket when the computer system has crashed, you will know about the chaos this causes. The checkout tills come to a standstill and, if the crash lasts for any length of time, you have to leave your trolley and walk out of the shop empty-handed!

One reason why the checkout tills cannot process the goods in the trolley is that none of the products are marked with the price. The bar code needs to be read in order to obtain the price of the goods from the computer. Computers also control stock levels and process customer payments at the tills.

Stock control – Computers control the amount of goods a store has

Bar code is scanned into the computer

5 010052 010037 >

Credit card – The electronic bill connects by networks to transfer money from bank accounts

Bank Name
Payment Card
4832 7390 5939 6140
VALID FROM   EXPIRES END
08 9 8   08 0 1
MISS JANE S TURNER
30-91-74   0883248
CODE NUMBER

Loyalty card – Encourage customers to return by awarding points, gifts and vouchers

CLUBCARD
234004 000452658 9720
NICO'S

The checkout till

Supermarket checkout tills are quite sophisticated with laser scanners to read the bar codes. They are also connected to the store's computer and so the till is given a special name in ICT:

- An ordinary checkout till is called a point of sale (POS) terminal.

- A checkout connected to a computer with a bar code scanner is called an electronic point of sale (EPOS) terminal.

- A checkout connected to a computer, with a bar code scanner, and which can transfer money from a customer's account using the customer's credit and debit cards is called an electronic funds transfer point of sale (EFTPOS) terminal.

As all modern supermarket checkouts will accept customer payments by plastic cards they are all technically called EFTPOS terminals.

Scanning and bar codes

All goods found on the shelves in supermarkets are labelled with bar codes. The bar codes are formed from a series of black and white lines of varying thickness and represent a 13-digit number, which is also printed under the lines. The number uniquely identifies the type of product and the 13-digits are divided into four groups of numbers showing the country of manufacture, the maker, the product number and a check digit.

Making sense of the bar code

The bar code can be read with a hand-held scanner or the laser scanner at the checkout. The scanner emits a beam of light that reflects off the bar code. The white lines reflect the light strongly while the black lines reflect less strongly. These variations in reflection are picked up by sensors in the scanner and converted into a digital signal.

Bar codes are cheap to produce (just part of the printing on the packaging) and can be read upside down and on curved surfaces.

If the bar code is damaged, the computer might read the number incorrectly and a tin of beans may be recorded as a bag of potatoes!

The final number of the bar code is a check digit which is calculated mathematically from the other 12 numbers. When the 13 numbers are read, the check digit is recalculated by the computer and if it is different to the character read by the scanner, the reader will not give the beep to indicate a successful scan. In this situation, the cashier at the till can enter the number manually.

The supermarket's computer holds a database containing information on all the products sold in the store. As the item is scanned, the bar code number is passed to the computer where a search is made of the database. As soon as the number is matched with the data held in the computer, the price and description are passed back to the till where the customer's itemised receipt is printed.

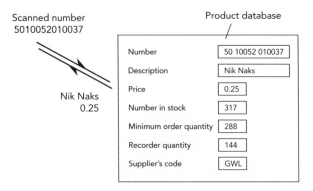

The bar code number is passed to the database from the till. The description and price of the item are then passed back to the till

Stock control

Keeping a careful check on the amount of stock in a supermarket is very important. If too many items are held in stock then valuable space is being taken up and there is also more chance of food going past its sell-by date. This is particularly important with so much fresh food now available in stores. Having too little stock can also cause problems for the store. If customers find that the goods they want are not available, they may shop in other supermarkets.

It is often the store manager's job to decide the amount of stock to hold in the store. In making these decisions, the manager will know how often new deliveries can be made and will have estimates of the number of customers likely to visit the store each day based on data from previous weeks. The manager's most important tool for controlling stock, however, is the store's computer.

As each item is scanned at the checkout, the bar code number is passed back to the database in the computer. One of the fields in the database record contains the number currently in stock. This number is decreased by one each time an item is scanned, thus giving the manager an accurate and up-to-date record of the current stock levels at any time.

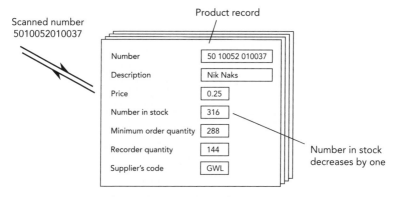

The number in stock has decreased by one

There are several other fields in the record that are held to maintain the correct stock levels. With the addition of these three fields, the whole process of stock control can be automated. These are:

- **Minimum order quantity** – This field holds a number that the manager has set as the lowest number the store should hold of an item. In this case the number of Nice 'N' Spicy Nik Naks packets should not be less than 288.

- **Reorder quantity** – When the quantity of Nik Naks packets falls below the minimum order quantity, this will be the number that are reordered.

- **Supplier code** – When the goods are to be reordered, the computer will use this code to locate the supplier's details and automatically generate an order for more packets of Nik Naks. This order will be transmitted electronically over the network direct to the supplier.

Special offers

Special in-store promotions like 'Buy two and get a third free' or 'Buy one and get a second one half price' are much easier to operate with the aid of computers. Details of offers are entered into the computer so that when the products are scanned, the offer appears automatically at the till and on the receipt.

The store's network of computers

The computers and computerised tills within the supermarket are connected together to form a local area network (LAN). The network server, normally located in one of the back offices, holds all the information about the products stocked in the store. This local area network will also be connected to a wide area network (WAN) so that data can be passed to suppliers and banks.

Loyalty cards

Tesco supermarkets introduced the first loyalty card in 1995. Now, the majority of supermarkets encourage shoppers to have loyalty cards for their stores. These are the plastic store cards with magnetic stripes that hold customer data and a unique customer number.

At the checkout, store points are awarded to the customer based on the value of the shopping or for particular items purchased with extra points included. This accumulation of points using the card can lead to cash and gift rewards that are designed to encourage customers to remain loyal to the store. However, the card also has other uses for the supermarket. When the customer presents the card at the checkout, the card details together with data of all the purchases made are stored on computer.

Supermarkets are investing millions of pounds in large mainframe computers with terabytes (terabyte = one million megabytes) of data storage. Computer software is then used to build a profile of the customer's buying habits and allows the supermarket to target customers with the aim of selling more goods. Sifting through large amounts of data in this way is also referred to as data mining.

Self-scanning

One of the potential bottlenecks when shopping at a supermarket is the checkout. Traditionally, the contents of the trolley are unloaded onto the conveyor belt and then need to be repacked after they have been scanned by the cashier. Supermarkets with self-scanners allow customers who hold loyalty cards to scan items using a hand-held scanner as they select goods off the shelf. These goods can then be packed directly into bags or boxes in the trolley and need not be unpacked again until the customer returns home. (This is a trust scheme and occasionally customers may have to have all, or part of their shopping rescanned at the till as a security check by the supermarket.) When the customer reaches the checkout

till, the hand-held scanner is passed to the cashier. The data held in the scanner is downloaded and an itemised till receipt printed.

Supermarket Internet shopping

Many of the large supermarket chains now have Web sites that allow customers to sit in the comfort of their own homes to do their shopping. Computer software is provided by the supermarket and this is loaded on the customer's home computer. When this program is run, a connection is made with the supermarket's Web site and the latest range of goods and prices are downloaded to the customer's computer.

The customer browses through the different categories of goods available. Items are grouped so that they can be located easily but a search facility is also available where products can be found by typing in the name. As the customer selects goods, they appear in the virtual 'trolley' ready for ordering. Goods that have been purchased before, from either a previous visit to the store or from earlier Internet orders are often highlighted to help customers find the goods they usually buy.

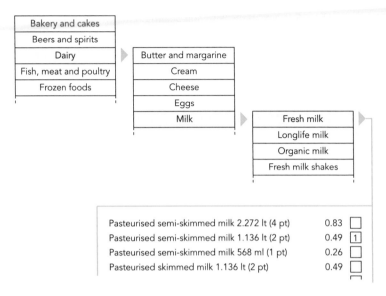

Selecting a bottle of semi-skimmed milk using hierarchical menu structure

When all the selections have been made, the order is placed. The computer again connects with the shop's Web pages and the 'trolley' details are passed to the shop so that the goods can be picked from the supermarket shelves. Payment for the order is made by credit card and a suitable delivery time selected for delivery.

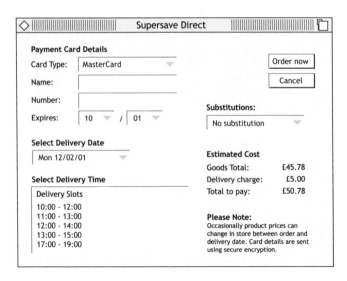

Tesco was one of the first supermarkets to introduce Internet shopping with home delivery from its stores. In 2000, it was the largest online retailer in Europe and during the year 1999 – 2000, Tesco's grocery orders rose from 15,000 to 60,000 orders – worth £5m – each week. During the same year, it created 7000 new jobs and extended the number of stores offering online shopping to 300. To cater for the half million online customers, the supermarket installed 80 Internet servers at a 'Web farm' where customers' orders from the Internet were processed and passed on through a computer network to the stores.

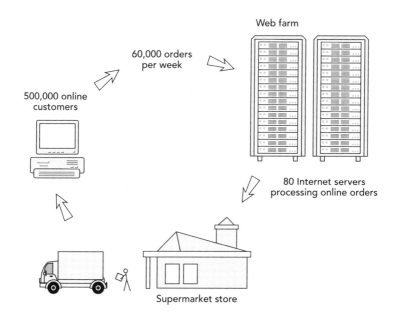

Web farm

60,000 orders
per week

500,000 online
customers

80 Internet servers
processing online orders

Supermarket store

1   Controlling the level of stock in a supermarket is very important. Give one reason why there should not be:

a   too much stock ....

b   too little stock ....

2   When a bar code is scanned at the checkout the bar code number is passed to a database in the computer where the price and description of the product are kept. The stock level for the product is also decreased and checks are made to see whether the product needs to be reordered.

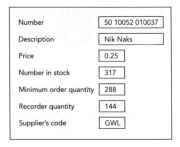

Number	50 10052 010037
Description	Nik Naks
Price	0.25
Number in stock	317
Minimum order quantity	288
Recorder quantity	144
Supplier's code	GWL

Arrange the following sentences into the correct order for this to happen. (The words in the [square brackets] are the contents of the fields in the database.)

A   Decrease the [Number in stock] by one.

B   If the [Number in stock] is less than the [Minimum order quantity] then

C   Pass back to checkout till the [Description] and [Price]

D   Order [Description], quantity [Reorder quantity] from supplier [Supplier code]

E   If scanned number is equal to the product [Number] then do the following instructions, otherwise look at the next record.

Correct order: E   ....

3 Supermarkets encourage customers to hold loyalty cards. When the card is presented at the checkout, points are awarded to the customer according to what they have bought. It is also possible for the supermarket to store details of the goods purchased together with the customer's details. In this way, the store can build up a profile of the customer. Match the till receipts below to the people by drawing a line to link each of them:

Customer A

*KODAK GOLD 200 36EXP	4.99
*KODAK GOLD 200 36EXP	4.99
*MOSQ REPELLENT	3.95
*R/SALTED CRISP	1.29
*STILL WATER 500ML	0.32
*STILL WATER 500ML	0.32
*ORAL B TYPE	1.89
*OASIS CITRUS 375ML	0.75

Customer B

*PEPSI S/FREE	1.29
*FANTA ORANGE	1.25
*MARS I/CREAM	1.99
*ARIEL ESSENTIAL	3.29
*5 CHEESE PIZZA	2.79
*BAKED BEANS X4	0.85
*BAKED BEANS X4	0.85
*BE COD F/FINGERS	4.49

Customer C

*BROCCOLI FLORET	0.99
*HONEYDEW MELON	1.49
*ORG RASPBERRIES	1.99
*SKIMMED MILK	0.49
*EGG TAGLIATELLE	1.69
*TRAY BAKING POTS	0.89
*ORG WHLMEAL	0.72
*ICEBERG LETTUCE	0.69

4 ICT in banks

Banks have a very long history of using computers. During the 1960s, all of the main banks had large mainframe computers installed to process bank cheques, keep records of their customer accounts and to calculate interest payments. This was 20 years before computers became generally available to smaller businesses.

Computers are perfect for processing and storing the millions of financial transactions that take place every day. Today, banks are using the latest technology to bring new services to customers.

Ways of paying for goods and services

For most people, the money they earn is paid directly into their bank account. In order to spend this money, it needs to be either taken from the bank or transferred from the bank account to pay for the goods and services. There are a number of common ways of doing this:

- **Cash** – Often obtained from the cash machine and generally used to pay for smaller items such as food, drink, bus tickets, haircuts, etc.

- **Plastic cards** – A very convenient way to pay for goods thus reducing the need to carry a large amount of cash. Often used to pay for the weekly food shop, petrol, clothes and goods purchased over the Internet.

- **Cheques** – Often used when paying bills by post or where sellers are not able to take plastic cards.

- **Direct debits/Standing orders** – Popular methods of payment where regular monthly and annual payments are made. For example, household accounts, Internet subscriptions and Sky Digital payments.

Cash

Automatic teller machine or ATM is the proper name for the cash dispenser or 'hole in the wall' machine which is used to obtain cash from the bank. To use an ATM, a bank card is inserted into the machine and the user is prompted to input their personal identification number (PIN) at the keyboard. If the PIN correctly matches the card, the user is offered a choice of services (see illustration on page 44). The card is then returned and the cash and receipt, if requested, follow.

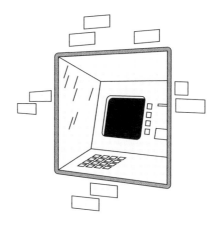

ATMs benefit customers because they are available 24 hours a day

All ATMs are connected to their own banks through a wide area network. The majority of the cash machines in the UK still use an older network that operates in a slightly different way to the Internet. When the user's card is inserted in the machine, data is read from the magnetic stripe on the back of the card. These details together with the choices the user makes are passed backwards and forwards between the machine and the bank's database holding the customer's information.

The financial investment of installing ATMs is huge. There are more than 25,000 machines currently in the UK and more are being installed every month. Each ATM is very expensive to make and install. As it is full of money, it has to be a small 'safe' with the addition of very precise electronic and mechanical mechanisms to dispense the exact amounts of cash requested. The machines must be built securely into the wall of a building with access to the rear of the machine for restocking it with money and the network connection to the bank.

At present the services available from the majority of ATMs are similar to those shown in the illustration above. As new machines are being installed, some banks are making use of Internet connections between the ATM and the bank. This makes additional services to customers possible. Already in the USA some ATMs offer postage stamps to customers. The ATMs of a Canadian bank offer cinema, theatre and airline tickets while in Cairo, users can pay their mobile phone bills by scanning a bar code on the phone bill at the ATM. Information can also be provided on the small screen and one bank in the UK already offers users reminders for birthdays and anniversaries!

All these additional services are possible but while people still need to queue up to obtain cash from the machine, the option of making them wait longer while someone at the front of the queue is processing cinema tickets could make the situation worse! Reducing the time customers spend at the machine is important to banks. Some banks download customer information into the ATMs so that the number of option choices offered to the customer is reduced. For example, when a user inserts their card in an ATM situated at an international airport, information stored in the machine about the customer would remove the need to ask which language to use when presenting the instructions.

With over 100 million bank cards in use in the UK and with over £5 million being withdrawn every day, ATMs play an important role in our day-to-day banking needs. The introduction of ATMs has led to large reductions in the numbers of staff working in the banks and has also made possible the closure of many village and small town bank branches. Closing local branches reduces the banks operating costs, making them more profitable in their competition with other banks.

Plastic cards

Plastic cards include the following:

- **Credit card** – This card allows users to make purchases and draw cash up to a pre-arranged amount. Each month the user receives a statement showing the purchases made using the card. The user can then decide whether to pay off all or part of the amount at the end of the month. Some credit cards, called affinity cards, allow the user to make a donation to an organisation, usually a charity, every time the card is used.

- **Debit card** – This card is linked to a bank account. When purchases are made using the card the money is taken (debited) directly from the account. Debit cards are also used to withdraw money from cash machines (ATMs) and, when used with bank cheques, the card guarantees that the cheque will be paid up to a specified value (ie £50, £100 or £250).

- **Loyalty card** – These are issued by shops and promote customer loyalty by awarding points for rewards or discounts. In some stores customers with loyalty cards are able to use additional services, for example, a loyalty card is required in Sainsbury's to use the self-scanning units.

- **Store card** – These are issued by shops and allow customers to make purchases in the store on credit. At the end of each month, a statement is send to the customer for payment. As with the bank credit cards, the customer can choose whether to pay off the full amount or only part of the money owed. If only a part payment is made, the remaining credit is extended to the next month and the customer is charged interest.

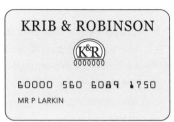

The use of plastic cards to make purchases and to obtain money from bank accounts has increased enormously since the cards were first introduced. Well over 80% of the adults in the UK have one or more cards and it is forecast that by the year 2005 there will be five billion purchases made annually with plastic cards. Internet shopping has also increased the importance of credit cards, as this is the most common form of payment for purchases made.

When credit cards are used to buy goods on the Internet or over the telephone, the customer's name and the numbers on the card are used. The details asked for include the cardholder's name, the card number and the card expiry date which is also printed on the card. For security, most companies will only deliver goods to the cardholder's registered address, this prevents goods being delivered to other people if the card is stolen.

Where the payment for goods is done at a checkout or the card is used to obtain money at a cash machine then the details on the card are processed electronically. On the back of the card is a magnetic stripe. The card data is held in digital form (0s and 1s) on the magnetic stripe in the same way computer data is held on a floppy disk.

The data from the magnetic stripe is captured as the card is passed through the machine and passed electronically to a computer.

For a cash machine, the data will be passed to the bank's computer for processing, whereas for a credit card purchase, the data is passed to the card company's computer. Where money is transferred electronically in this way it is called electronic funds transfer (EFT). The checkout till, for example in the shop or garage, where the purchase is being made is called a point of sale (POS) terminal. If the checkout till has the equipment to swipe plastic cards and transfer money electronically, it is called an electronic funds transfer point of sale (EFTPOS) terminal.

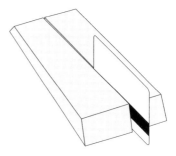

Card reader capturing data from the magnetic stripe

With well over 100 million plastic cards being used in the UK it is necessary to try to stop card fraud by criminals. The three greatest areas involving plastic card fraud are:

- cards being lost or stolen

- cards being copied (counterfeit)

- payments made over the telephone or Internet when the card is not present.

When a person realises that they have lost their cards or have had them stolen it is very important to contact the bank and the credit card companies straightaway. Details of the lost and stolen cards can then be broadcast electronically to cash machines and point of sale terminals in shops so that the cards can no longer be used. A lot of effort has been put into upgrading checkouts (EFTPOS) terminals so that lost and stolen cards can be detected in this way.

Another way that has been used effectively to stop lost cards from being used is lowering the 'floor' limit in shops. This is the amount a customer can spend when using their card before the shop is required to seek authorisation from the credit card company. This means when they phone for authorisation, the shop can be notified if the card is lost or stolen. By introducing these checks and also providing shops with better training and advice, the level of fraud from lost and stolen cards has fallen and criminals have turned to making counterfeit (copying) cards.

The use of small hologram images makes the cards more difficult to copy. Also, the introduction of tiny microchip processors or smart cards makes the data on the card virtually impossible to copy (see the next section). Counterfeit card crime in 1991 accounted for only 3% of fraud losses, but the losses have been doubling every year since 1998.

The graph below shows the rise in card fraud between 1998 and 2000:

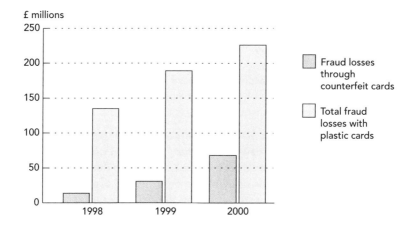

Plastic cards with chips

In order to make plastic cards more secure against fraud and also to give them more functions, a tiny integrated circuit is embedded into a card. The standard for this integrated chip card, or ICC, (also known as a 'smart card') was agreed by all the major banks in 1998 after extensive trials of the card. The silicon chip, which will eventually replace the magnetic stripe on the card, contains a processor and memory. Conductive pads on the card enable input and output data to flow from the card reader to the chip.

A 2 cm square chip – cushioned in epoxy resin. Wires lead from the chip to the gold contact panels which make the connection when the card is read

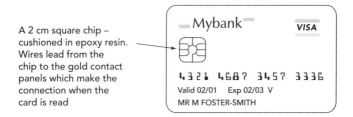

Storing data in the memory of the chip makes it much more difficult for criminals to copy cards or amend the data. Integrated chip cards will still have a magnetic stripe so that the cards can be used on older point of sale checkouts in shops but over the next few years terminals in retail shops will be upgraded to read the new cards.

Cheques

Cheques are still a common way of paying for goods although the number of cheques being used is gradually reducing as debit and credit cards are used more. In 1998, three billion cheques were processed but this is expected to fall to 1.9 billion by 2008. Blank cheques are issued to customers by banks and, although they may seem to be just a piece of paper, they are in fact a legal document which allows the account holder to pay a specified sum of money to the person or organisation named on the cheque. Cheques are not a new idea, they were first used towards the end of the 1600s.

Three billion cheques a year represents almost 100 cheques being written every second of every day. With so many cheques it would be impossible to process the information without the use of computers and so a special method was devised for inputting the data into the computer. Because cheques involve the transfer of money, the data input used had to be very reliable. The method devised uses an ink holding tiny magnetic particles which can be read directly into the computer through a reader. This method of data entry is called magnetic ink character recognition (MICR).

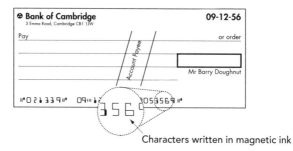

Characters written in magnetic ink

Payment by cheque is still common for paying bills over the counter or by post and for payments between businesses.

The illustration above shows three groups of magnetic ink numbers printed on the bottom of the cheque. These numbers represent:

- the cheque number (each cheque in the cheque book is stamped with its own number)

- the sort code for the account holder's bank (each bank and branch has its own unique number)

- the customer's bank account number.

Before the cheque is passed for processing, also known as 'clearing', a fourth number is added by the bank using a printer with the special magnetic ink. This last number is the amount the cheque has been made out for.

The processing, or clearing, of cheques in Great Britain is managed by the Cheque and Credit Clearing Company Limited. When a customer takes a cheque that they have received to the bank, it takes three days for the cheque to be cleared and the money made available to the customer to spend. The process of clearing a cheque is outlined below.

SNOOKER TABLE

6x4 ft, excellent condition, less than a year old, cues, scorer and balls included. **£35**.
Contact Mr Jones: 01244 232987

David finds a snooker table advertised as a private sale in the local newspaper. David and his Dad, Mr Williams, visit Mr Jones and purchase the table

Day 1

- Mr Williams writes out a cheque and gives it to Mr Jones in payment for the snooker table.

- That afternoon Mr Jones pays the cheque into his bank.

- The bank prints the amount onto the bottom of the cheque (in this case £35).

- That evening the cheque is passed to the bank's local clearing house.

- The cheque is scanned and data is passed electronically over a secure data network (called the Inter Band Data Exchange, IBDE) to the paying bank clearing centre – in this case Mr Williams' bank.

- (Mr Jones' bank balance will increase by £35 but he will not be able to spend this money until the cheque has been cleared.)

Day 2

- Mr Williams' cheque is taken from the local clearing centre to the central exchange centre together with the other cheques. (Here all the cheques are swapped ready to be returned to their original banks.)

- Mr Williams' cheque is collected and taken back to his bank's clearing house.

Day 3

- The bank staff look at all the cheques that have been presented for payment. They decide whether to pay the money or not. If the bank decides not to pay a cheque, it is returned and the cheque is said to have 'bounced'.

- If Mr Williams' bank agrees to pay the cheque then £35 will be deducted from Mr Williams' account.

- The £35, plus any money from other cheques that is owed to Mr Jones bank by Mr Williams' bank is added up and sent electronically to the Bank of England. The same is done at Mr Jones' bank for money owing to Mr Williams' bank. Then, the difference, or the net value, is transferred electronically through the Bank of England.

- Mr Jones' bank now clears his money so that he can spend the £35.

As you can see, processing a cheque, or rather nine million cheques a day, is quite a complex operation. All the cheques are sorted by computer using magnetic ink character recognition on the bank sort code, with all the cheques being returned by road and rail to the local clearing houses.

Automated payments

So far we have dealt with making or receiving payment with cash, plastic cards and cheques. Many payments, however, are set up to run automatically by linking the banks computers to the Bankers' Automated Clearing Service (BACS) computer centre in London – the largest automated clearing house in the world.

These automated payments fall into two types:

- **credits** – paying money **into** our accounts
- **debits** – paying money **from** our accounts.

Paying money into accounts

Direct credits are made by business to individuals or other businesses. The majority of the payments made each year are from paying wages, salaries and pension contributions.

An example is where a business pays the monthly salaries of its staff. The process of paying direct credits takes three days. On the first day, the business electronically transmits a datafile containing a list of the staff, their bank account details and salary payments to BACS. During the second day, BACS processes this data and passes details of which accounts should be credited (receive their salary payments) over a secure network to the banks. On the third day, the staff receive their salaries and the business has the money removed from its account.

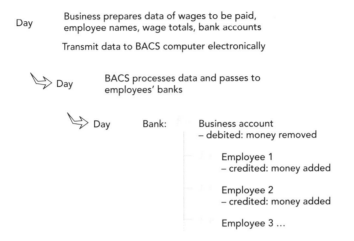

Day — Business prepares data of wages to be paid, employee names, wage totals, bank accounts

Transmit data to BACS computer electronically

Day — BACS processes data and passes to employees' banks

Day — Bank: — Business account
– debited: money removed

Employee 1
– credited: money added

Employee 2
– credited: money added

Employee 3 ...

The process of paying salaries by BACS

In 2000, there were 1,100,000,000 direct credit payments made through BACS. 50% were wages and salaries.

Paying money out of accounts

When people have bills to pay on a regular basis, eg every month, these can be paid using direct debits and standing orders. When you complete a direct debit form, it gives the bank the authority to make regular payments direct from your bank account to the organisation you specify.

In the case of standing orders, the amount the customer pays is fixed. Direct debits are more flexible as the amounts taken from the individual's account can change. For example, a direct debit would be better for paying a telephone bill as the amount varies each month. When the amount varies, the customer is always notified at least ten days before the money is taken from the bank account.

Direct debits are used to pay subscriptions, household bills (gas, electricity, oil, water rates, council tax), rent, insurance premiums, loan and rental payments

Benefits

Direct debits are popular with customers because paying bills automatically saves the time and trouble of sending a cheque or paying cash. Businesses receiving the money also benefit, as they know exactly when the money is transferred into their account.

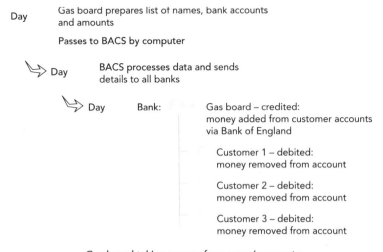

Day   Gas board prepares list of names, bank accounts
       and amounts

       Passes to BACS by computer

Day   BACS processes data and sends
       details to all banks

Day   Bank: Gas board – credited:
                money added from customer accounts
                via Bank of England

                Customer 1 – debited:
                money removed from account

                Customer 2 – debited:
                money removed from account

                Customer 3 – debited:
                money removed from account

Gas board taking money from users' accounts

1   A press release issued in September 2000 by Association for Payment Clearing Services (APACS) said:

"UK CARD FRAUD LOSSES SURGE BY OVER 50%,
with counterfeit fraud growing by 104% to £68 million. The most worrying counterfeit method involves copying genuine data from the magnetic stripe on one card, without the cardholder's knowledge and putting it onto another card – this is called skimming."

a   What method is currently being used to stop counterfeiting (copying) plastic cards?

....

....

....

b   Why will it take several years before this solution can be used all over the country?

....

....

....

2   Complete the sentences below by choosing the correct words from the following list:

   debit   credit   clearing   banks   funds   package

For many workers in Britain their salaries are paid directly into their bank accounts through a direct .... system. BACS (the Bankers' Automatic .... Service) are based in London and have powerful computers which transfer millions of pounds of funds between ....

3 Many terms in computing are shortened to using the initials only (called an acronym). The following have occurred in this chapter. Write out the words in full next to the acronym:

ATM ....

PIN ....

EFTPOS ....

ICC ....

MICR ....

BACS ....

4 Four types of plastic card are described below. Match the description to the type of card by drawing a line to link them:

Issued by shops and used to collect
points for rewards of discounts •   • Credit card

Allows purchases to be made in
shops, garages and over the Internet •   • Store card

Used to withdraw money from cash
machines and used to guarantee cheques •   • Loyalty card

Issued by shops to allow customers to
make purchases in that particular store •   • Debit card

Computers have been used by the police force for many years in their fight to combat crime. Back in 1974, the Police National Computer (PNC) at Hendon came online to hold data about criminals and to link with the Drivers Vehicle Licensing Agency computer to provide vehicle information for police forces around the country. Much has changed since that time due to the huge advancement in information technology systems and many new systems are currently being trialled and implemented across the country.

Coordinating and developing police systems

In England and Wales there are 43 local police forces. For many years these individual forces developed their own information technology systems. Although many of these systems worked well, they were not always compatible with the systems developed in other areas, or with the Police National Computer, and so information could not be shared easily.

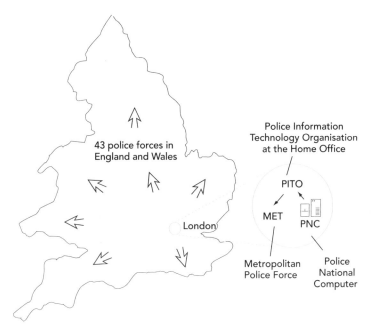

Structure of the police force regarding ICT

In 1994, the National Strategy for Police Information Systems (NSPIS) was launched. This strategy set out the future for ICT development across the police force giving a coordinated set of standards for sharing and communicating data. The strategy also proposed the development of national software that could be used by all police forces. Two years later, in 1996, the Police Information Technology Organisation (PITO) was set up as part of the Home Office in London. The role of PITO is to coordinate the development of ICT within the police force by supporting the National Strategy. By working with the ICT industry, PITO is currently developing and delivering systems to local police forces across the country as well as national schemes. PITO is also responsible for supplying police forces with information from the Police National Computer.

Police National Computer

The Police National Computer, situated at Hendon in London, serves all the police forces around the country. A new computer was installed during the 1990s. It is a mainframe computer, made by Siemens, with enormous processing potential and data storage. It is linked to police stations and mobile terminals in police patrol cars across the country and deals with an average of 65 million transactions a year.

The computer holds a number of databases but the main two are on criminals and vehicles.

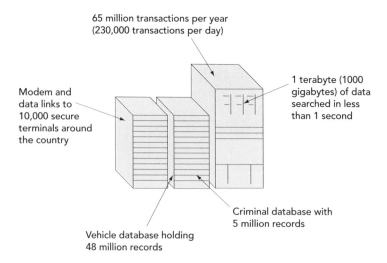

65 million transactions per year
(230,000 transactions per day)

Modem and data links to 10,000 secure terminals around the country

1 terabyte (1000 gigabytes) of data searched in less than 1 second

Vehicle database holding 48 million records

Criminal database with 5 million records

The Police National Computer

Also at Hendon is another very powerful computer running the Automated Fingerprint Identification System. The processing power of this system, which checks the digital images of fingerprints, is equivalent to half a million computers that we might use in school or at home.

Gathering information

When a crime is reported the details are entered into a computer. One piece of software currently used by the police force for this task is CRIS – a Crime Reporting Information System. Details of the offence, the victim, witnesses and suspects are all entered. With the data stored electronically, it can be accessed by other police forces and the data can even be combined with computerised mapping systems to identify clusters of particular crimes.

Criminal database

For everyday police work it is vital for police officers to be able to access information on known criminals. The information held includes:

- a personal description
- last known address
- details of the offence committed
- methods used to carry out the offence
- details of the arrest
- previous convictions and prison sentences
- known aliases
- known accomplices.

This database is held on the PNC computer in Hendon and is known as PHOENIX, which stands for Police and Home Office Extended Names IndeX. This database is online 24 hours a day and can be used by police officers around the country. Descriptive searches can be used to match to criminals in seconds.

Other databases

As well as the criminal database, other databases are held by the police including:

- **Vehicle database** – This is the largest database held on the Police National Computer with over 48 million records of vehicles and their owners. The data is constantly updated by the Vehicle Licensing Authority that handles all the vehicle licences. With the latest software called Vehicle Online Descriptive Search (VODS), officers around the country can receive results within seconds of vehicles matching the partial descriptions given by witnesses. Over 24 million enquiries a year are made from this database.

- **DNA** – The DNA molecule is the biological building block of life and the structure of each person's DNA is unique. In the same way that fingerprints found at the scene of a crime can lead to a conviction so too can minute samples of DNA when analysed and coded by the forensic team. In the autumn of 2000, the police DNA database reached one million records.

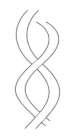

- **HOLMES** – This stands for the Home Office Large Major Enquiry System. For major crimes, such as murder, large amounts of data are collected by the police. This software coordinates the information and looks for similarities with other cases. The latest software, HOLMES II, enables all the data on the PNC to be accessed and it is able to suggest new lines of inquiry based on the data fed into the system.

- **Stolen property** – This is a project known as GRASP – Global Retrieval, Access and information System for Property! The development of this database is being led by Scotland Yard in London with European funding. The database can be accessed worldwide and its aim is to help police trace high value stolen property. A police officer investigating a theft will key in a description of the stolen property. The software will then dial up the

different databases in each country and will return a small digital image of the property that appears to match the description. Selecting these images then produces a full size picture and a description of the object.

Fingerprints

When it comes to proving identity, fingerprints still provide the main evidence. The use of matching fingerprints found at the scene of a crime were first used by the police in 1901 although an article describing the "unchangeable finger furrows of important criminals" was outlined in the publication *Nature* in 1880. Every person's fingerprints are unique and remain unchanged throughout their life. Exactly 100 years after the introduction of using fingerprints, all police forces are due to go online with the latest computer software for matching prints. This project, known as NAFIS – National Automated Fingerprint Identification System, can compare fingerprints with those stored in the computer at a rate of a million per second.

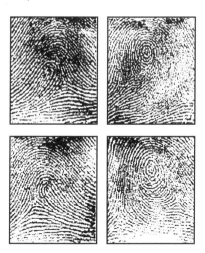

Fingerprints found at the scene of the crime are photographed and scanned into a computer terminal. The software compares the prints with the stored images in the PNC database and returns the best matches. A fingerprint specialist then examines the results from the computer to make the final match. Tests have shown a matching accuracy greater than 99%.

The database currently holds 4.6 million sets of ten prints (eight fingers and two thumbs), a total of 46 million images. It is capable of holding nine million sets of prints, which makes it one of the largest image databases in the world. This database is also the first in the world to link directly to a criminal record database (see PHOENIX on page 59).

Nottingham was one of nine police forces involved with the initial trials of the NAFIS software. Unfortunately for one criminal, within two hours of the new system being switched on, the police were able to make a positive identification of his fingerprints found in a stolen car.

With the huge advance in the technology of mobile telephones it is not surprising that police officers are being equipped with the latest radios to combat crime. The new police radios come with extra features you would not find on models in the high street. From the keypad on the radios, officers can directly access criminal and vehicle databases held on computer and both the voice and the data signals are securely encrypted making them safe from eavesdroppers. The officer's location on patrol can be monitored at the police station and an emergency button on the radio can be used to summon help. The radio network also provides wide national coverage allowing officers to communicate with other forces across the country with a strong, clear signal.

Automatic number plate recognition

If the police wish to check the details of either a vehicle or its owner then they can look this up in the database of vehicles on the computer. Each record in the database uses the vehicle's registration number plate as a unique field. Traditionally, the police officer would use the radio to contact the police station to request a vehicle check. The vehicle registration would be entered at the terminal in the station and the details of the search radioed back to the patrol officer.

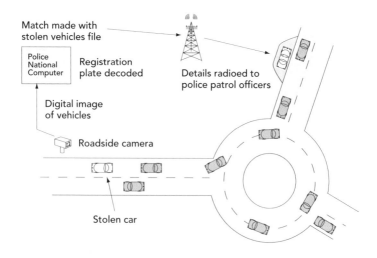

Automatic number plate recognition

Now, with the advances in digital image decoding software, vehicle registration plates can be recognised by the computer as they pass a camera. These cameras are mounted by the roadside and in the back of police patrol vehicles. Full details for every vehicle are returned from the computer in seconds and, if matches are made with stolen or suspect vehicles, details of the vehicle's location are passed directly to police patrol vehicles. More than 100,000 vehicle checks can be processed each day using this system.

Questions

1   What do the following terms stand for:

   a   NAFIS? ....

   b   CRIS? ....

   c   PNC?..

   d   GRASP?..

   e   HOLMES? ....

   f   PHOENIX? ....

2   Where is the Police National Computer based?

   ....

3   Which has more records, the vehicle database or the criminal database?

   ....

4   Complete the following sentences by choosing the correct words from the list below:

   criminal   second   million   eight   compare

   A powerful police computer holds 4.6 .... sets of fingerprints

   with each set consisting of ten images (..................... fingers and two

   thumbs). The computer software can search through the database and

   .... fingerprints at the rate of one million per ....

   The fingerprint database is also linked to the .... database

   so that when a fingerprint match is found, details of the suspect are

   also presented.

5   In order to demonstrate to students how the police might use a criminal database, a teacher prepares the following table of 'suspects'. For each of the statements below, identify a possible suspect using the names in the table:

Surname	Forename	Eye colour	Hair colour	Height	Age	Vehicle registration
Wetton	Nicholas	Blue	Brown	180	22	W255 DER
Williams	Christopher	Brown	Black	176	29	A318 PTW
Hooper	Joe	Blue	Blond	153	41	E477 HOG
Hunter	Michael	Green	Red	170	32	FTG 363D
Johnson	James	Blue	Brown	171	34	G213 CAT
Troy	James	Brown	Black	185	28	P254 JAT
Cooper	David	Brown	Brown	178	32	W441 FJR
Robinson	Carl	Green	Bald	156	48	X570 PRG
Ellis	Noel	Brown	Black	150	23	E665 RDV
Lingane	Liam	Blue	Blond	164	28	G436 TRX

Suspects database — File Edit Format Insert Tools Window Help   4 March 2001 5:32 pm

95K used   record 1 of 10

a   The suspect had red hair ....

b   The suspect was very small and had dark hair ....
....

c   The suspect was a blond man driving an 'E' registration car ....
....

d   The suspect had blue eyes, dark hair and was in his early 20's ....
....

e   The suspect had green eyes and was driving a modern car ....
....

f   The suspect had brown hair, or perhaps it was his eyes that were brown, anyway, he had a personalised number plate on his car
....

Making and selling cars is a very competitive industry. Over recent years many of the smaller companies have gone out of business or have been taken over by the well-known car giants like the Ford Motor Company. Modern ICT systems are used in the industry to improve efficiency, lower costs and increase sales. Without investing in ICT systems, companies would not be competitive in the marketplace.

Car manufacture

From the point where the motor manufacturer's research and development team come up with a new idea for a car, ICT is involved in every process of making the vehicle. The first stage involves using the computer design software to produce 3D (three-dimensional) images of the new car. CAD (Computer Aided Design) software is used to produce accurate scale drawings for all the components that make up the vehicle. These drawings include the exact dimensions and materials needed and this information is then passed from the design software to the computerised machinery that make the parts. The linking of the design software through a network to the manufacturing machinery is known as CAD/CAM (Computer Aided Design/Computer Aided Manufacture). Often parts are made by other companies and shipped to the factory to be assembled. When this happens, the data on the parts needed is passed to the 'third party' company.

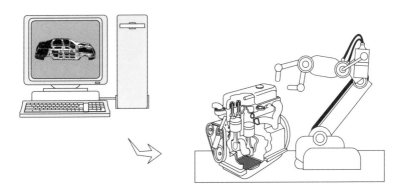

Product is designed on CAD system, the data is transferred to Computer Numeric Control (CNC) machines, and the product manufactured with CAM

Many parts are needed to make a car so the factory that assembles them often extends over a large area and is divided into smaller zones where the different processes take place. If engines are being made then one area of the factory will have furnaces where molten metal is poured into moulds to cast the main engine blocks and cylinder heads. These parts will then move to the next area for machining and assembly with the other engine parts. The car itself will start with the pressed sheet panels that form the body of the car. These panels are welded together and the body of the car moves from the weld to the paint area. Here, the shell of the car is immersed in anti-corrosion paint and dried by heaters before the additional layers are spray-painted on.

After this the car is assembled; the interior, seats, dashboard, engine and suspension units, the wheels and windows until the finish vehicle comes off the assembly line ready for testing. Throughout this build process the car passes through the different parts of the factory on conveyor systems. Robots controlled by computers perform many of the tasks including welding the panels, handling and assembling parts and paint spraying. A large car plant may have over a thousand computerised robotic machines involved in the building and testing of the cars.

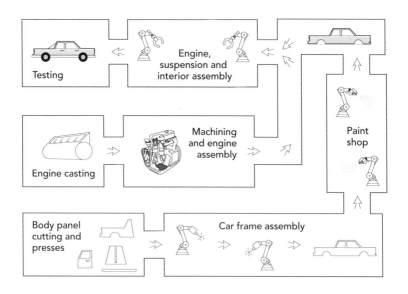

Processes involved in car manufacture

A robot is a mechanical device that can be programmed by a computer to perform a variety of tasks. Robots come in all shapes and sizes depending on the type of work they will be used for. The illustration below shows some of the features of an industrial robot.

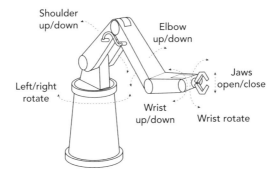

Industrial robot showing the six degrees of freedom

To give robots the greatest flexibility of movement they are designed so that they can rotate around a number of axes. These are called 'degrees of freedom' and the most common type are the six degrees of freedom shown in the illustration.

An actuator is the name given to a device that generates physical movement from a computer data signal. Three types of actuator are commonly used to control the movements of a robot. These are:

- **Hydraulic systems** – Here, the output from the computer controls the movement of hydraulic rams by pumping oil through pipes. These hydraulic rams, similar to those seen on mechanical diggers, are very powerful and can handle large and heavy objects. Robot movements based on hydraulic systems are slower than pneumatic and electrical systems.

- **Pneumatic systems** – These are similar to hydraulic systems in using rams but the pistons are powered by air rather than oil. Pneumatics are not as powerful as the hydraulic robots but the movements are much faster.

- **Electric motors** – The most common type of electric motor used in controlling the movement of robots is a stepper motor. These motors rotate an exact amount for each pulse of electricity sent to the motor and provide very precise movements for the robot.

Robots can be classified as follows:

- **First generation** – These are programmable robots but they lack any input sensors so they are unaware of their surroundings. For example, if a robot was programmed to spot-weld the panel of a car but the car was not positioned correctly then the weld might take place in mid-air. The use of first generation robots in car assembly lines meant that the car frame had to be positioned with great precision on guide tracks, which was in itself an expensive thing to achieve. In computer control when there is no feedback of data to the computer, this is known as an **open loop system**.

- **Second generation** – These robots include sensors that feed data back to the computer making them 'aware' of their surroundings. These might include proximity (how close to objects) sensors, light and heat sensors or strain gauges that measure small changes in pressure and might stop the robot from gripping an object too hard. In computer control where there is feedback to the computer, this is known as a **closed loop system**.

- **Third generation** – These are the latest robots under development in research laboratories that can 'learn' on the job. Robots operate under artificial intelligence software and can adapt and reason with the incoming data to improve their own performance.

Why use robots?

There are many advantages to using robots in manufacturing processes, including:

 They can operate faster than humans.

 They do not get tired and need to sleep, eat or have breaks.

 The quality of the work is consistent.

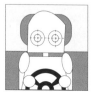 They do not lose concentration and make mistakes.

 They can carry heavy loads and their arms can reach long distances.

 The running costs are very low in comparison with workers' wages.

 They can work in environments that are hazardous to humans.

Of course, not all robots are used in manufacturing cars; they now have many uses across a variety of industries. The first robot was used in 1962 at the General Motors factory in the United States. Since that time the manufacturing industries of Japan have led the world in terms of the numbers used. In 1998, there were 10,800 robots in use in UK manufacturing, this is estimated to grow to 15,000 by 2002 when the total number of robots worldwide will reach 800,000.

Robots, like all ICT equipment, have improved in performance while prices have fallen. A modern industrial robot with six axes of movement and controlled from Microsoft® Windows software can now be purchased for between £20,000 and £30,000. 15 years ago the cost would have been nearer ten times this figure.

Car production and sales

The traditional approach in car manufacturing plants uses 'mass production' techniques. The aim is to produce as many cars as possible from the factory production lines in the shortest time and car workers on the shop floor are rewarded for any increase in productivity (increasing the number of vehicles made). The cars rolling out of the factory are usually parked, row after row, in huge compounds waiting until they can be shipped to dealers and sold. There are, however, disadvantages with this method of production including:

- Large amounts of money are tied up in the thousands of cars waiting to be sold.

- Customers buying cars are becoming increasingly particular about the options they require. It is quite possible, even with the thousands of cars waiting to be sold, that a car matching the customer's specific requirements may not be available.

'Not-at-all' manufacturing is a new approach to car manufacture that is gaining popularity around the world. It was used for the first time in the motor industry by the Japanese. With this system the car manufacturer designs the car but other, third party, companies make the parts. The parts are then shipped to the car plant where the car is assembled. This method of 'not-at-all' manufacture is already well established in the manufacture of other products, eg for making computers and printers. Using this system to manufacture cars enables a customer to have a car delivered from the factory within five days of specifying their exact requirements.

This new method of manufacture can reduce the cost of cars by nearly 30% compared with the traditional mass production methods. The car is only made to a customer's order so there is no stock piling of unsold cars. The car manufacturer also saves money through not having to store and stock the parts needed in the manufacturing process.

The whole process, which is based on advanced integrated ICT systems, is illustrated below.

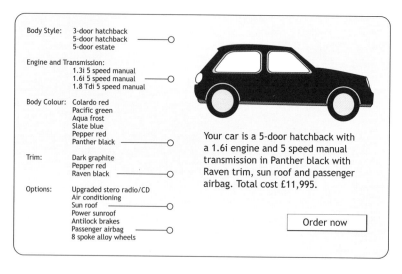

A customer configuring their car over the Internet

Day   The customer configures their
       personal specification for the
       car on the Internet.

       The company checks the order
       and passes details to 'third
       party' suppliers.

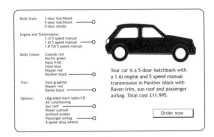

Day   Third party suppliers manufacture
       the parts required.

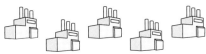

Day   Parts delivered by
       suppliers to car company.

Day   Car company assembles car with parts
       delivered from different suppliers.

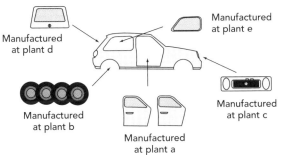

Day   Car delivered to customer.

Supplying spare parts to dealers

Car manufacturers use dealers, both across the country and worldwide, to sell their cars to the public. The dealers also repair and service the cars and, in order to do this, they will hold stocks of spare vehicle parts. It is important for the dealers to hold the correct type and the correct quantity of spare parts but this is not an easy task to achieve. If too much stock is held then money has been spent unnecessarily and extra space is needed for storage. If too little stock is held then customers have to wait longer for servicing and repairs to be carried out while stock is ordered. They may even have the inconvenience of having to bring their cars back to the dealer twice or more for the repairs to be completed.

The problem of 'what' and 'how much' stock to hold has been tackled by one car manufacturer in a different way. Instead of the dealer requesting stock, the manufacturer's central warehouse has taken the responsibility for ordering and replenishing stock to the dealers. This system is called a 'supplier-managed inventory' and operates in the following way:

- At the end of each day a datafile is produced at the dealer's with details of the parts sold that day. This is passed over the Internet, using a secure encrypted connection, to the central warehouse where the data from all the dealers is collected. The warehouse can also access the current stock levels in each dealership.

- The software in the warehouse computer then gives each product a rating based on how many have been sold on a national basis. It then generates a suggested list of parts that each dealer should receive to replenish its stock.

- The suggested order is sent back over the Internet to the dealer where the manager can amend the list and confirm the order. This confirmed list is returned to the warehouse where the goods are picked and despatched to each of the dealers.

Using this system has resulted in lower stock levels at the dealerships but with more of the correct parts being stocked. Because of the more efficient system, the number of emergency and daily supplementary orders received at the central warehouse has also decreased.

1   Robots use three types of actuators – devices that change the data
    signals from the computer into physical movement. These actuators are
    hydraulic systems, pneumatic systems and electric motors. Which type
    of actuator might be chosen for robots in the following situations?

    a   Performing hip replacement surgery in a hospital.

    ....

    b   Handling the huge rolls of paper needed for newspaper
        printing presses.

    ....

    c   Performing a rapid series of spot-welds along the edges of
        car panels.

    ....

2   A press release issued in summer 2000 stated:

    "Rocketing Robot Sales – UK Automotive Industry Snap Up Over Twice
    The Number of Robots Purchased Last Year – UK robot sales figures for
    the second quarter of 2000 are the best for over two years and show an
    increase of 127% on this time last year with a total of 412 robots sold."
    Give one reason why you think this may have happened.

    ....

    ....

3   Complete the following sentences by choosing the correct words from
    the list below:

    two-dimensional   *aided*   *data*   *manufacture*   *drawings*

    Computer .... Design software is used to produce accurate
    scale .... for all the components that make up a vehicle. The
    software can create three-dimensional images from flat ....
    drawings and include the exact sizes and materials needed. Once the
    drawing is finished, ... is sent directly to the computer-
    controlled machines that manufacture the component. This is called
    Computer Aided ....

4   Explain the main difference between first generation robots and second
    generation robots.

    ....

    ....

The health service uses ICT in many different ways. This includes assisting with hospital administration and enhancing the communication between doctors and nurses. ICT also plays a vital role in the diagnosis, treatment and care of patients.

Patient records

When a person visits their doctor or goes to the hospital, the details of their injury or illness together with the treatment they receive are recorded in the person's medical record. Until quite recently all of these notes were recorded on paper and kept in the patient's medical record folder. During the next few years many of these notes will be entered into databases on the computer and by 2004 it is estimated that three-quarters of hospital records will be kept in this way.

Paper records

Storing medical records on paper has a number of disadvantages. As records for a patient are kept and added to for the duration of their lives, medical folders can become very bulky. This makes the search for information in the folder quite time-consuming. Also the completion of the records by the doctors and nurses requires a lot of time to be spent with paperwork. Large hospitals hold millions of records for patients that need to be stored. These paper-based records take up large amounts of room and many clerical staff need to be employed to retrieve and file the folders as well as sending records on to other hospitals when patients move. With so many folders to look after there have also been cases of records being lost over the years.

Holding medical records for patients on computer solves many of the problems encountered with the paper-based folders. Doctors and nurses can enter the data more quickly using structured forms and data can be retrieved in a fraction of a second. Records do not have to be fetched manually from storage but can be retrieved instantly through networked workstations from inside the hospital or even from other hospitals and surgeries around the country. This allows hospitals to reduce their costs by employing less clerical staff. Also, records held on magnetic disks occupy a fraction of the storage space required by the paper systems.

A patient's file contains sensitive medical and personal information that must be kept safe and secure from unauthorised access. Access to records from workstations on a computer network is made using usernames and passwords. This allows different users to have varying levels of access to the data within the records. For example, administration staff would only have limited access to the data whereas doctors would be able to view the more sensitive data.

Holding medical records on computer provides the additional advantage of checking the combinations of drugs prescribed to patients. In the event of a doctor prescribing a new medicine to a patient, a computer program can check the database to ensure that the new medication can be taken safely with other drugs that the patient may already be taking. Combinations of certain drugs can cause serious problems for patients when taken together. With so many drugs now available, the ability of the computer to check the combinations of different medications is a valuable tool for doctors.

The government is planning to introduce a system where people will carry a copy of their medical records around with them. This would be achieved by downloading the medical data into the memory of a tiny computer integrated circuit embedded into a 'smart card'. Banks are already making extensive use of these cards to hold account information and to protect against fraud. A medical smart card could provide vital information for doctors in the event of a sudden illness or accident. (See page 49 for an illustration of a smart card.)

Monitoring patients

When people are very ill or have been involved in serious accidents they are placed in the intensive care unit of the hospital. Here, equipment with built-in microprocessors is used to help the nurses and doctors monitor vital body functions of patients. Using special input sensors, data from a patient is passed to the computer. If this data falls below or above set limits that have been programmed into the computer, an alarm is triggered. The diagram below illustrates this for the electrical activity of the heart.

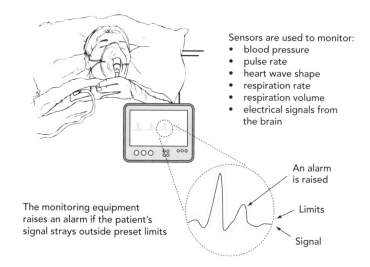

Sensors are used to monitor:
- blood pressure
- pulse rate
- heart wave shape
- respiration rate
- respiration volume
- electrical signals from the brain

An alarm is raised

The monitoring equipment raises an alarm if the patient's signal strays outside preset limits

Limits

Signal

The computerised monitoring equipment in the intensive care department allows the patients to be monitored constantly. Without such equipment each patient would require their own dedicated nurse every second of the day and, even then, changes in the patient's condition could not be detected as quickly or as accurately.

Special care baby unit

When babies are ill or have been born early they may have difficulty with breathing and feeding. In special care baby units, babies are placed in incubators that provide a constant temperature and help to protect them from infection. The air inside the incubator can be enriched with oxygen and ventilator machines may also be used to help the baby breathe. The baby's progress must be watched constantly and sensors linked to computerised monitoring equipment collect data on heart rate, temperature and blood pressure. Readings are taken and input to the computer every second, 24 hours a day. If any readings are received that fall outside the limits programmed into the computer, an alarm is sounded to summon a nurse.

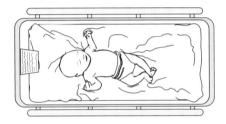

Computers are often used to detect or diagnose illnesses. Data from sensors attached to the patient can be fed into a computer. The data is then analysed and the computer will indicate potential problems or display the results graphically for a doctor to see. For example, to test for heart disease a patient may have sensors attached to their chest and to a monitor while being made to exercise hard on a treadmill. A consultant heart specialist can then examine both the printed heart trace and the computer monitor to detect defects in the electrical signals from the heart.

Another important piece of hospital equipment is the computerised axial tomography (CAT) scan machine. The CAT scan involves a narrow beam of X-rays passing through the body in thin slices and from different directions. The signals from the X-rays are fed into a sophisticated computer that builds up a three-dimensional picture of the internal organs of the body. CAT scans enable safe, rapid and painless diagnosis of parts of the body that were previously inaccessible and are used to detect tumours, cancer, brain and spinal cord disorders.

Medical training

Computers are used to assist in the training of doctors and nurses. For example, the diagnosis of some medical conditions can be very complex

77

and difficult to learn. The symptoms of a disease may be well known but the way it manifests itself can be different in different patients. As part of a doctor's training, computers are used to describe and show the different symptoms of diseases so that doctors can practise diagnosing the illnesses.

To help with training, simulation software of the human body can show the function of nerves, the circulatory system and the immune system. The computer can simulate the effect of drugs on the body to show how long they are active in the bloodstream. It also shows the effect of different doses and the need for repeated doses at specific intervals.

It is vital that doctors have knowledge of the latest medical information and techniques. This is less of a problem for new doctors leaving university than for established doctors but the government is introducing a National electronic Library for Health (NeLH). This library is due to come online in 2002 and will provide easy access to the best current knowledge and know-how. One of the aims of the library is to become one of the 'greatest medical libraries in the world' to help all health care professionals.

Operational and administrative tasks

Computers play an important role in the administration of a hospital. With thousands of people being admitted every day, computers are used to print labels for patients' belongings, their medical charts, wrist bands and test samples containers. Computers are used to make hospital appointments and the computer software can generate mail-merged letters to patients. Booking system software is also used to ensure the most efficient use of the limited resources in the hospital, for example CAT scan equipment and operating theatres. Computers are used to assist in purchasing supplies for the hospital and for maintaining the stock levels of goods including drugs and medicines.

With patients arriving and departing daily, organising the food is one of the huge tasks undertaken in a hospital every day. One way in which this task can be helped by computers is to use cards where patients make their choice from the menu by marking the card with a small line. Just like selecting the numbers on a lottery card, the patients' menu choice cards are input directly into the computer using the input technique known as Optical Mark Recognition (OMR). The different ingredients for each dish on the menu are known and so when all the cards have been read, the computer can calculate the total quantities required. These figures are then sent over the Internet to the food supplier who delivers the correct quantities of ingredients to the hospital kitchens.

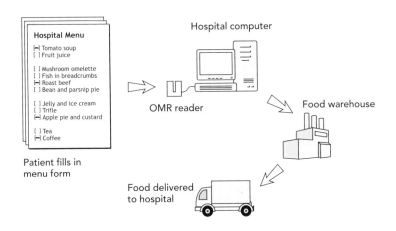

Hospital Menu

[⊞] Tomato soup
[ ] Fruit juice

[ ] Mushroom omelette
[ ] Fish in breadcrumbs
[⊞] Roast beef
[ ] Bean and parsnip pie

[ ] Jelly and ice cream
[ ] Trifle
[⊞] Apple pie and custard

[ ] Tea
[⊞] Coffee

Patient fills in
menu form

Hospital computer

OMR reader

Food warehouse

Food delivered
to hospital

For medical workers who visit patients at home, the National Health Service Trust supplies pocket computers that hold up to 2000 patient records in their memory. The records held on the pocket and on the surgery computers are synchronised when the worker returns to the office. Hence any changes made to patient records in the surgery are passed to the pocket computer and changes made while visiting patients at home update the surgery computer. This process of synchronisation should be able to take place immediately, or in 'real-time', with the next generation of Internet-based mobile phone devices.

NHSnet

For many people, a visit to the local doctors' surgery when they have a problem may only be the start of their treatment. They may then need to be referred by their GP to a consultant doctor at the hospital or they may need to have further tests carried out. In the past, the usual way in which surgeries and hospitals communicated was by putting a letter in the post. This, of course, is much slower that using modern networked communication systems and so the NHSnet system was started.

NHSnet is a major project to connect all the computerised doctors surgeries around the country to a private computer network linked with hospitals. The project was started in 1996 and is ongoing to provide a fast and secure method of transferring data between surgeries and hospitals. By 2002, it is expected that many surgeries will be able to book hospital appointments for their patients directly over the network from the surgery.

NHSnet can also be used for referring a patient to another doctor or requesting and receiving the results of laboratory tests. By 2005, it is hoped that the electronic patient and health records will also be available to surgeries across the NHSnet.

NHS Direct

NHS Direct is a service that allows the public to have access to medical information directly. Initially, over 150 public access points were set up. These terminals are easy to use with touch screen operation and are situated in schools, universities, health centres, supermarkets and holiday resorts around Britain. You can also access the service by telephone or over the Internet. The NHS Direct Web site provides a wealth of information on health features, healthcare, conditions and their treatments and even audio clips to listen to on health topics. The service, which is backed up by trained nurses 24 hours a day, has been very successful with as many as 100,000 hits (people accessing the Web pages) per day.

Questions

1   The medical records of patients are being moved from being stored on paper in folders to being held digitally on computer disk. Describe two advantages of holding medical records electronically.

i   ....

ii ....

2   Complete the sentence below by choosing the correct words from the following list:

two-dimensional   technology   organs   skin
three-dimensional   detect   blood   tomography

Hospitals use CAT (Computerised Axial ....) scans to build

.... images of the .... in the body. CAT scans

are used to .... tumours and cancer.

3   Three major ICT projects that were started to help modernise the NHS are described below. Match the descriptions on the left with their short names on the right:

Allows the public access to medical
information directly, either over   •   • NHSnet
the telephone or through the Internet

Connection of all the computerised
surgeries and hospitals through a   •   • NHS Direct
private computer network

The electronic library with access to
the latest medical information and   •   • NeLH
techniques for health care professionals

4   In some hospitals, OMR forms are used to collect information each day on the food patients would like for their meals. Each patient would complete their menu selection by making a mark on the form against the menu items of their choice.

[ ] Cheese salad   [ ] Apple pie

[~] Roast beef   [~] Fruit salad

[ ] Bean and parsnip pie   [ ] Cheese and biscuits

The forms are then collected and the data input directly into the computer using an OMR reader. In addition to inputting data about the food choices, explain what other data must be input from each form.

....

....

....

5   A sensor monitoring a patient's heart activity is sending signals to the computer every 5/100ths of a second. The computer checks to see if the reading received is between the upper and lower limit set.

a   Complete the table by placing the values from the incoming data stream into the table between the upper and lower limits. (The first two values have been inserted for you.)

Incoming data stream ⟶ First value

2.4	2.5	2.6	3.6	3.8	3.0	2.5	2.0	8.0	5.1	3.0	2.6	3.0	2.5	2.5

Upper limit	2.6	2.6	3.2	2.7	3.2	5.2	8.1	2.1	2.6	3.1	3.9	3.5	2.7	2.6	2.5
Incoming data	2.5	2.5													
Lower limit	2.3	2.3	2.8	2.5	2.8	5.0	7.9	1.9	2.4	2.9	3.7	3.3	2.5	2.3	2.2

b   Highlight the value that falls outside the upper and lower limit that would trigger the alarm.

c   As each data value is received from the heart sensor it needs to be compared with the upper and lower limit. Which of the following statements will correctly trigger the alarm if the incoming value is outside the limits? Note < means less than; > means greater than.

i   If 'data value' > 'lower limit' OR 'data value' < 'upper limit' then trigger alarm.

ii   If 'data value' < 'lower limit' AND 'data value' > 'upper limit' then trigger alarm.

iii   If 'data value' < 'lower limit' OR 'data value' > 'upper limit' then trigger alarm.

....

You may have learnt in History about the Industrial Revolution where people flocked from the countryside to find work in the towns and cities. Now, the information technology revolution is reversing that trend by allowing people to move away from the towns and cities and work from home in the country. The number of people working from home instead of the office has been rising steadily. In July 2000, 1.2 million people in the UK were home working and this number is forecast to double by 2003 to 2.4 million (10% of the UK workforce). What makes home working possible are the advances in ICT. The cost of the equipment necessary to work effectively from home is affordable for many employers and the advantages to both the worker and the company can be considerable.

The diagram below illustrates some of the equipment that might be used for home working.

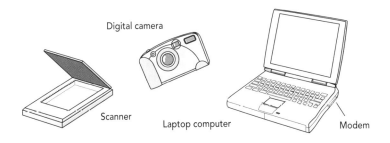

Digital camera

Scanner

Laptop computer

Modem

Being able to communicate with the office, work colleagues and, in some cases, with customers is vitally important. A fast way of accessing the Internet for receiving emails, video conferencing and connecting to the office intranet (see page 85) can be achieved through ISDN, ADSL and broadband connections.

Why work from home?

Working from home has improved the quality of life for many people. They no longer have to spend hours travelling to work, sitting in traffic jams or relying on public transport. They can avoid the noise and bustle of the city office and, instead, enjoy the comforts of home. Usually, working hours can be more flexible to fit in with other commitments, for example taking children to and from school. There are also good reasons for the employer to encourage home working. When new staff need to be recruited it may not always be possible to find staff with the right skills living locally or willing to travel to the office. Home working makes it easier to recruit staff with the right skills from anywhere in the country and removes the need to pay high salaries and relocation expenses. The increase in the quality of life offered by home working is important to workers and they will often accept lower salaries in exchange. Companies also save money by having smaller offices; the saving in city office space can be as much as £6000 per worker per year.

Some of the advantages and disadvantages of home working for both the worker and the employer are as follows:

Advantages to the home worker:

- Improved quality of life.
- No stress of travelling to the office.
- Travelling time saved.
- Cost of travelling saved.
- Greater flexibility of working hours.
- Increased self-esteem by being trusted to work at home.
- Can be at home with children.

Disadvantages to the home worker:

- Possible feeling of isolation.
- No social contact with fellow workers.

Advantages to the employer:

- Saves cost of office space.
- Greater loyalty from employees because of the trust given to them.
- Often workers increase the amount of work they do from home – increased productivity.

Disadvantages to the employer:

- More difficult to build teams and share and generate ideas between colleagues.
- Additional cost of home working equipment and connection charges for employees.

Employers need to provide the right facilities to make home working effective. One problem for workers is the feeling of isolation when they operate from home. Employers can use video conferencing over the Internet so that workers can interact more effectively. Web pages with company information and news can also be created for workers to access from home. These Web pages, which are held on the company's computer and are only used within the organisation, are called an intranet.

Security

When companies have Internet connections into the internal network it is very important to protect against unauthorised access by hackers. Some companies issue biometric devices, like thumbprint scanners, to home workers to use instead of relying on passwords when logging on. Home workers browsing the Internet are also more likely to pick up viruses because they will have less protection on their computers than the office systems. Employers need to ensure their home workers have the latest anti-virus software installed on their machines.

Questions

1   Complete the following sentences by choosing the correct words from the list below:

isolated   home   people   less

school   greater   trust   stress

Working from .... has improved the quality of life for many

people. It removes the .... and cost of travelling to work

and gives .... flexibility of working hours. Some

.... do find working from home difficult, as they are

.... from their colleagues.

2   With the advances of ICT, more people are now able to work from home rather than the office.

    a   List three pieces of ICT equipment that would help people to work from home.

....

....

....

b   List three advantages of home working for the worker (employee).

....

....

....

3   A fast Internet connection is often essential for home workers. List two types of computer Internet connection they could use.

....

....

Buying a used car from a garage or through a private sale can be fraught with dangers for the average person because they are not experienced to see any potential problems with the vehicle. For this reason, many people like to arrange for the vehicle to be inspected by independent experts before making a purchase. The RAC provide such a service with a team of trained engineers across the country that are able to visit and carry out 160 different checks on the vehicle for sale and provide the potential buyer with a detailed report.

Original manual system

Up until 1988, before they were issued with computers, the RAC engineers received details of their daily appointments by telephone or by voice mail messages. At the site for the inspection they would complete handwritten forms while carrying out the necessary vehicle checks. A copy of the report could then be left with the customer if they wanted one immediately and the other copies of the report were posted back to the office where the details were entered into the computer and filed.

There were certain areas of this operation that caused some difficulties. Often, the weather conditions during the inspection could be awful and the handwritten forms were damaged by wind and rain. Delays were encountered in getting the forms back to the office through the post. In the office, the staff employed to enter the reports into the computer could make mistakes reading the engineer's handwriting and also the cost of employing the data entry staff was considerable, particularly with the number of inspections continuing to grow each year. It was recognised by the company that the quality of service and the efficiency of the inspection operation could be improved with the introduction of ICT.

The ICT solution

After careful and detailed research of the systems available on the market, the RAC engineers were issued with personal digital assistant (PDA) computers. The current system has menu-driven software and electronic forms displayed on the tablet screen. It is easy for an engineer to enter the results of an inspection while it is taking place. Data is entered using a pen and the computers are protected for rugged use with a waterproof, hard-wearing shell. A mobile phone and portable printer to use with the computer are also provided.

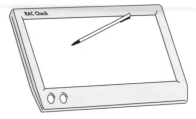

Handheld computer as used by RAC inspecting engineers

With the new system, the engineers are able to print a report for the customer using the mobile printer directly after completing the inspection. The inspection details are also transmitted electronically to the office using the mobile phone attached to the computer, so avoiding the delays of posting paperwork. Because reports no longer need to be entered into the computer at the office, both the data errors and 'data entry' staff costs have been reduced.

The new system also handles the engineer's appointments more efficiently. When a customer rings to book a vehicle inspection, the details are entered into the computer at head office. Inspections are then allocated to

Vehicle Examination Checklist

Body Exterior						
1 Panel Condition/ Alignment	☐	☑	25 Engine Mountings	☑	☐
			26 Fuel Injection	☐	☑
2 Paintwork	☐	☑	27 Turbo/Super Charger	☑	☐
3 Exterior Trim	☐	☑			
4 Glass	☑	☐	28 Fuel Pump/Pipes	☐	☑
5 Bumpers/Number plates	☐	☑	29 Accelerator Linkage	☑	☐
6 Door Locks/ Operation	☐	☑	30 Body Panels	☐	☑
			31 Bonnet Catch	☐	☑
7 Fuel Filter Cover/ Petrol Cap	☑	☐	32 Bonnet Hinges	☐	☑
8 Soft Top (operation/ condition)	☐	☑	33 Cold Starting	☑	

Customers are able to have a detailed printed report of the inspection immediately

engineers and the details of the inspection (date, time, address, vehicle details, etc) are sent electronically to the engineer's computer. The new system saves time, has reduced phone call charges and is more flexible by allowing last minute changes to be made when allocating the inspections to the different engineers.

In 2000, the RAC were asked to carry out nearly a quarter of a million vehicle inspections. With the introduction of ICT, the company has been able to improve the quality of service to customers as well as reduce the amount of paperwork and costs to the company. ICT solutions also enable services to be enhanced. A development of this system might include keeping a database of known weaknesses in different makes and models of cars. This would enable additional checklists to be downloaded into the engineers computer specifically for the car being inspected.

Questions

1   Complete the following sentences by choosing the correct words from the list below:

> *vehicle   computer   head office's   electronically*
> *date   year   customers   printed*

When .... ring to book a vehicle inspection, the data is

entered into the .... computer. This data includes details of

the .... together with the customer's name, address, time

and .... of the appointment. The appointments are then

allocated to the engineers and the data is passed .... to

each engineer's computer.

2   The engineers that carry out inspections are issued with a small computer called a PDA.

a   What do the letters PDA stand for?

....

b   List two modifications that have been made to this computer to stop it being damaged when used at the roadside.

....

....

c List two other peripheral devices that are issued with the PDA computer.

....

....

3 On average, how many vehicle inspections did the RAC carry out each day in the year 2000?

....

4 By providing the RAC engineers with portable computers to use for their task of inspecting vehicles, they were able to reduce costs in the company and improve the quality of service for customers. Give one example of:

a a reduction in company costs.

....

....

b an improvement in the quality of service for the customer.

....

....

A call centre is a place offering help and support to people. The call centre may need to help customers, staff or members of the public. For example, it could be a call centre:

- for a company to deal with customers' questions and problems about the goods it sells
- inside a company to help support different departments, for example, an ICT support centre
- for a local council that needs to provide help on a range of issues, from questions on refuse collection to council tax payments.

Before ICT systems

Before the use of ICT integrated systems there was only a telephone link between the customer and the member of the call centre support staff. The customer often experienced long delays before the phone was answered and the problem solved. If the problem could not be solved on the first call, when the customer called again they would usually find themselves speaking to another person and would have to explain the whole problem again. Customers only phoned because they had problems and so they were often irritated, angry or upset even before they had been kept waiting on the phone! For the support staff, the combination of dealing with difficult customers all day and having a job that was generally not well paid led to experienced staff leaving and being replaced by new, inexperienced staff. This made a difficult situation worse.

With integrated ICT systems

There have been two major changes in the development of call centres, the attitude of companies towards customer service and the development of technology. With the intense competition between companies, managers have realised that good customer service is vital. A company may spend millions of pounds on advertising but if a customer receives poor service when they contact the company then that customer may never return to purchase goods or services from them again. This commitment to handling customers' problems efficiently and effectively has led many companies to make much greater use of ICT equipment.

Modern call centres

Customers can phone, email or fax their problems to the call centre. Customers are also encouraged to browse the Web site where a database of technical information is often available and answers to the most frequently asked questions (FAQs) are posted up by the call centre staff. Call centre staff also have access to the Internet and the same database of information from their networked computer workstations. Allowing customers and staff access to the same technical information avoids customers receiving conflicting information from different sources.

Call centre staff enter details of the customer's call into the computer using a software package that tracks and monitors the problem until it is solved and the call is closed. This means that if customers call in again and speak to different staff, details of the problems and the progress taken towards its solution are available onscreen. This saves the customer from having to repeat their problem to the new member of staff. The call centre software prompts staff to contact customers and keep them informed of the progress being made and includes useful management software to monitor the speed and effectiveness of service being given to customers.

Managing a call centre is a stressful job but it has been made easier with the use of ICT and greater emphasis on staff training.

Specialist call centre software monitors and tracks a customer's problem from start to finish

Question

Complete the following sentences by choosing the correct words from the list below:

   FAQ   help   stressful   information   integrated   email   track

Call centres offer .... and support to customers.

.... ICT systems allow call centre staff to obtain solutions to customers' problems from large databases of .... and they can also .... the progress of a customer's problem. Customers are also encouraged to visit the Web site and read the ....

The object of air traffic control (ATC) is to ensure that aircraft are safely separated from each other, and from obstacles on the ground, during their entire flight. The airspace above the UK is one of the most congested in the world. As well as flights from Europe flying over the UK, there are millions of people flying in and out of the country. London Heathrow is the busiest international airport in the world. There are also four additional London airports – Gatwick, Stansted, City and Luton. With the other major airports of Birmingham, Manchester, East Midlands, Liverpool, Leeds, Newcastle, Edinburgh and Glasgow, there can be 5000 flights a day for air traffic control to manage safely.

Air traffic controllers must ensure that aircraft stay well clear of each other. Using information from their radar screens the controllers can instruct pilots to alter their course, to climb or descend. Between any two aircraft that might conflict, the controllers ensure that they have either a vertical separation of 1000 feet (about 300 metres) or are separated by ten miles. Ten miles may seem a large distance but two aircraft approaching head-on and travelling at 600 miles per hour would impact in 30 seconds. At these speeds, by the time the pilot sees an approaching plane it is too late to take evasive action. It is for this reason that controllers are vital for the safe passage of aircraft.

*Air traffic control
tower*

The controllers spend much of their time watching the movement of aircraft on the radar screens. They work in darkened rooms and during busy times they are only permitted to work for two hours at a time because of the intense concentration needed. Each aircraft, displayed as a 'blip' on the screen, is tagged with information that includes the flight code, speed (in knots), flight level and course direction. The computer systems linked to the radar data constantly calculate the movement of the aircraft. By using the direction, speed and height of the aircraft, the computer software calculates the path and indicates a warning to the controller of any conflict situations. The controllers have radio contact with the pilots of all the aircraft they control and will direct them to alter their course when necessary.

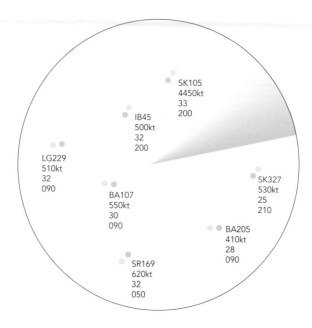

Calculations are performed automatically by both the computer and the controller to ensure no two aircraft enter the same air space

National Air Traffic Services Ltd (NATS)

All air traffic over the UK land and surrounding seas is managed by NATS, the National Air Traffic Services Ltd. As well as operating controllers at airports, there are other centres that control aircraft that are travelling ('en route') to their destinations. A new NATS En Route Centre at Swanwick in Hampshire is due to become operational in 2002. The Swanwick Centre will operate a mainframe S/390 computer to process all the flight data and distribute this to air traffic controllers around the country. Every aircraft must file a flight plan before setting out. These flight plans are entered into the computer and the Flight Data Processing System (FDPS) program passes details over the computer network to the air traffic controllers involved. NATS is also responsible for the provision and maintenance of the radar, navigation and communication systems required by air traffic control. The figure on page 95 illustrates how different controllers become involved as an aircraft arrives at an airport.

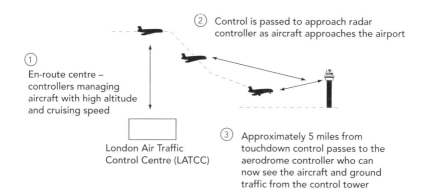

① En-route centre – controllers managing aircraft with high altitude and cruising speed

② Control is passed to approach radar controller as aircraft approaches the airport

London Air Traffic Control Centre (LATCC)

③ Approximately 5 miles from touchdown control passes to the aerodrome controller who can now see the aircraft and ground traffic from the control tower

Radar

There are two main types of radar used to track aircraft – primary and secondary:

- Primary radar is the traditional form of radar where a beam of energy is transmitted from the radar dish. When the beam strikes an aircraft, the energy is reflected back to the radar dish providing data on the direction and distance of the aircraft.

- Secondary radar relies on each aircraft being fitted with a small transmitter/receiver called a transponder. Each aircraft is allocated a four-digit code that is keyed into the transponder. The ground radar station transmits a request to the transponder in the aircraft that replies by transmitting the unique code together with data on the aircraft's height. The code is checked against the flight plans held in the computer to obtain the flight code and destination of the aircraft.

The data from the primary and secondary radar systems are combined on the radar screen to provide the air traffic controllers with all the information they require to manage the aircraft safely to its destination.

Ground radar stations are located across the UK and throughout Europe. As the radar scanner rotates, data is collected continuously and fed through a computer network to all air traffic control centres. The different European countries have agreed on a standard format for this data so that it can be exchanged across country boundaries. This common exchange format is called All purpose STructured Eurocontrol Radar Information eXchange (ASTERIX). The European-wide network for the distribution of radar data is called RAdar Data distribution NETwork (RADNET) and ensures that each air traffic control centre can extract the radar data for the area of their operations.

Questions

1 Air traffic controllers operate from all the major UK airports. List five major UK airports including two London ones.

   ....

   ....

2 What do the following acronyms stand for:

   NATS? ....

   ATC?...

   FDPS?...

   RADNET? ....

   ASTERIX?..

3 Complete the following sentences by choosing the correct words from the list below:

   > maintenance   S/390   NATS   communications
   > Swanwick   flight

   The new .... en route centre is due to become

   operational in 2002. The centre, based at .... in

   Hampshire will house the mainframe .... computer that

   processes all the .... data. NATS is responsible for the

   provision and .... of the radar, navigation and

   .... systems required for safe aircraft control.

4 The illustration below shows an air traffic controller's radar screen. The controller is responsible for the seven aircraft shown as blips on the screen. Each aircraft is identified on the screen by a code letter, A to G. The details below the code letter show:

- the speed in knots
- the flight level in thousands of feet, eg 30 x 1000 ft = 30,000 ft
- direction, eg 90 = East, 180 = South, 270 = West, etc.

a On the illustration below, mark the two aircraft that are on a collision course and mark the place of impact if the controller takes no action to avert the disaster.

b Which other aircraft might be a cause for concern and what instructions should the air traffic controller give the pilot of this aircraft?

....

....

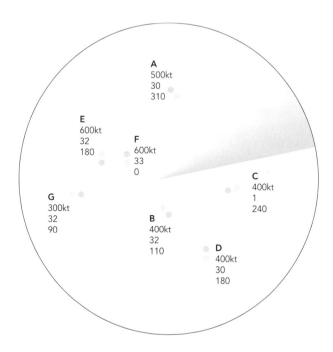

12 ICT in weather forecasting

The weather is an important subject for many people. When two acquaintances meet their opening remarks will often refer to the state of the weather. We might look at the weather forecast in order to plan a day out or what to do at the weekend, but for some organisations an accurate forecast can be critical to plan their operations and can even save lives. For example, airlines must be aware of severe weather and the possibilities of ice and snow at airfields. Even with regular daily flights, airlines can save money by getting pilots to fly at altitudes that avoid strong head winds and so use more fuel. Fishermen and sailors check the shipping forecasts frequently to ensure they are not caught at sea in high winds or storm conditions. Farmers need to plan their work according to the weather and look particularly at the five-day forecasts for tasks such as harvesting crops. The Environment Agency and river authorities need detailed information in wet weather so they can activate flood defences and issue flood warnings in good time and everyone should be aware when severe weather warnings are issued.

People have tried to forecast the weather ever since they began to depend on agriculture and fishing for their livelihoods. For most of the last 3000 years this forecasting has been based on weather lore, for example, 'Red sky at night, shepherd's delight' or 'Rain before seven, fine by eleven'. Although this weather lore had some scientific basis, it was very limited. In 1922, a man called Lewis Richardson developed the first numerical weather prediction (NWP) system. His model divided the atmosphere into grid cells and applied complex calculations to each cell. In order for his weather forecast to have been made he needed a 'forecast factory' as he called it with 64,000 people each performing a part of the calculation with a mechanical calculator. There were no computers in the 1920s and so any calculations to forecast the weather always took too long. In one recorded case, a forecast for the next eight hours actually took six weeks to calculate!

The Meteorological Office (Met Office) in Bracknell, Berkshire had access to their first computer in the 1950s. This was the LEO 1, a valve computer built by Lyons, the caterers. They then purchased their own computer in 1959 and were able to use the numerical forecasting methods devised by Lewis Richardson. Because of the large amounts of data being processed, there has always been the need to have the most powerful computers available. Since 1959, the Met Office has upgraded their computer system five times. The latest system, installed in the late 1990s, is two Cray T3E Supercomputers. These are the second and third most powerful computers in Europe for weather forecasting (Germany has the fastest Cray T3E system in Offenbach).

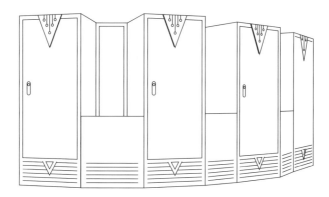

The Cray Supercomputer used by the Met Office to forecast the weather

Sources and collections of data

A huge amount of data is collected every day to assist in forecasting the weather. One meteorologist (a person who studies the weather) calculated that the amount of data being collected and used to forecast the weather now was 170,000 times more than the amount of data used 25 years ago.

The weather data is collected from land-based stations, from out at sea, from the air and from orbiting satellites. This data is usually collected using automated instruments with their own embedded microprocessors. The data is stored in memory before being passed on to larger computers for processing. The important weather data collected includes:

- the temperature
- the wind speed (constant and gusts)
- the wind direction
- the air pressure
- the humidity (amount of water vapour in the air).

The illustration on page 100 shows a typical land-based automated weather station containing an embedded computer to record and store weather data.

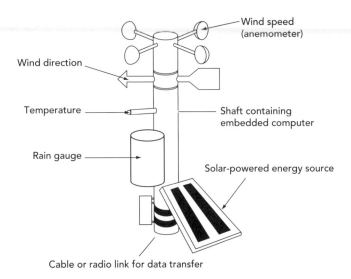

Automated weather station

Different sensors are used for each of the items being measured. Some sensors, for example the thermistor that measures the temperature, are analogue devices. The materials that make up the thermistor change their resistance to the flow of electricity as the temperature changes. The warmer the air, the less the resistance and so more electricity can flow. These constantly changing electrical readings that are recorded as the temperature rises and falls are called analogue readings.

Analogue readings must be changed to digital readings before they can be input to a computer. This is done with an electronic device suitably called an analogue to digital (A to D) converter.

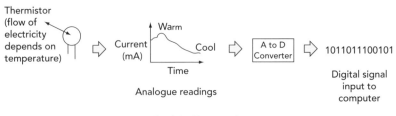

An A to D converter

As well as land-based weather stations, data is also gathered from a number of other sources:

- Weather balloons are released daily from many locations around the world. Each balloon is fitted with a miniature radio transmitter called a radiosonde. Weather data, including temperature, humidity and pressure are broadcast from the balloon at fixed heights as it rises up through the atmosphere.

- Infra-red cameras mounted on orbiting satellites also transmit valuable weather data back to earth. Geostationary satellites (those orbiting with a speed to match the earth's rotation so they are always located above a fixed point) monitor the movement of clouds. Polar orbiting satellites provide temperature data.

- Radar stations feed large amounts of weather data through for processing. A special kind of radar, called Doppler radar, is used to track rain and clouds as they move through the atmosphere. Radar is also used to track weather balloons as they rise through the air. Tracking the balloon gives information on the wind direction and speed at the different altitudes.

- Weather data is also provided from instruments on aircraft and from ships and buoys out at sea. The ocean temperatures and currents have a large effect on the world's weather and this data is also recorded and passed for processing.

In order to forecast the weather, a computer program has been made to model the behaviour of the atmosphere. The model involves making large numbers of very complicated calculations using the enormous quantity of data being input to the computer. The Met Office supercomputer, the Cray T3E, uses a Massively Parallel Processors (MPP) system with 700 processors each working on calculations. For the computer forecasting model, the surface of the earth is divided into a two-dimensional grid. The calculations involved for each cell in the grid are then allocated one of the processors in the supercomputer. Each processor is capable of making up to 600 million calculations per second.

The power of a supercomputer is measured in flops (floating point operations per second). Floating point calculations mean performing calculations on fractions and non-integer numbers which are quite complex operations for computers. The power of the Met Office supercomputer with 700 processors is around 400 gigaflops (1 gigaflop = 1,000,000,000 floating point calculations per second). The fastest supercomputer in the world runs at 4.9 teraflops (1 teraflop = 1000 gigaflops). The next generation of supercomputers are being planned to operate in the petaflop range (1 petaflop = 1000 teraflops or 1,000,000,000,000,000 flops).

With the increased power of the new Cray computer, the climate model is being improved to include more links between the ocean currents and the atmosphere. Also, the effects of aerosols and chemicals in the air are being incorporated into the model for greater accuracy. Although the accuracy continues to improve, the mathematical models run on the computer cannot represent every geographical feature that might cause a local variation in the weather.

Presenting the weather forecast

Over the years, weather presenters on television have used various methods to help them illustrate their broadcasts. Before the use of computers, a picture of the UK was displayed on a board behind the presenter. As the weather forecast was being given, the presenter would turn to the board and place magnetic symbols in the appropriate parts of the country to show the sun, clouds, rain and snow. These symbols were then moved across the board to illustrate how the weather would change.

Computers are now used to project images onto the screen. At the touch of a button, the computer images change to show the winds, temperatures, pressure lines (isobars) and even satellite images. These can be presented like a slide presentation, smoothly moving from one picture to another or as moving animated images.

1 List four different sources that are used to obtain weather forecasting data.

....

....

2 Complete the following sentences by choosing the correct words from the list below:

operations   *Cray*   *Met*   *gigaflops*   *computer*   *five*

Since the purchase of their first .... in 1959, the

.... Office in Bracknell has had ....new systems.

The latest is a .... T3E supercomputer with a performance of

400 .... (flops stands for floating point .... per second).

3 a List four types of weather data collected by a land-based automated weather station.

....

....

  b Describe how this might be passed to larger computers for processing.

....

....

4 The performance of supercomputers is measured in flops (floating point operations per second). Link the prefixes below to the number of quantities of flops shown on the right:

Petaflops •   • 1,000

Kiloflops •   • 1,000,000,000

Megaflops •   • 1,000,000,000,000,000

Teraflops •   • 1,000,000,000,000

Gigaflops •   • 1,000,000

13 The future

There have been many predictions about the future of ICT. The following examples illustrate some of the forecasts for developments over the next few years.

"India is set to become the next IT superpower"

In the year 2000, the Indian software industry generated $8 billion in revenue. With 350,000 software engineers, 100,000 more than the United States, it is predicted that by 2008 the revenue from computer software will grow to $87 billion. India's pool of talent is growing faster than any other English speaking country with more than 67,000 computer software professionals leaving college every year.

"Bluetooth set to revolutionise communications"

Bluetooth wireless technology provides short-range wireless links between equipment. The small radio module will enable digital signals to be sent between mobile phones, computers, printers and scanners without the need for wire connections. From the 11 million units fitted with bluetooth shipped in 2000 it is forecast that this will grow to 671 million units by 2005.

"Invisible computers are seen as the future!"

The speed and power of the processors in computers continues to increase without any sign of stopping. The one billion instructions per second (1000 mips) barrier has been passed and by 2005 it is expected that processors performing three billion instructions per second will be commonly available. These processors will be fast enough to process speech input so that no eye or hand contact will be needed. For example, you will be able to say "Book me a weekend in Stockholm at the best price" and the computer, using the Internet, will complete all the arrangements for you.

"Frozen chips but not for eating!"

Fridges and freezers will be developed that monitor the freshness of food. Computer chips inside these appliances will be able to suggest menus based on the food available and will be able to reorder food using their own mobile phone Internet connections.

"Switched on clothes"

Shoes, especially thick-soled trainers and platforms, are seen as the ideal article of clothing to house a computer. They have plenty of room for a chip and lithium-polymer batteries. Polymer screens will be sewn onto sleeves and data will flow through electro-active threads. A person's clothes will become a personal area network.

"Moore's law runs out"

In the 1960s, Gordon Moore stated that the power of computers doubled approximately every 18 months. At the time, he was not predicting the future but making an observation on the development of computers since the 1940s. As computer power has continued to follow the same growth pattern up until the present day his statement has become known as Moore's Law. Of course, for computers to develop in this way there have been fundamental changes in the hardware technology. Modern computers use integrated circuits but before this transistors and vacuum valves were used. As there is a physical limitation on the silicon integrated circuits in today's computers it is forecast that his law will end around 2010 unless a new technology is invented.

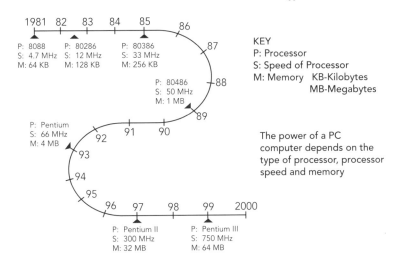

KEY
P: Processor
S: Speed of Processor
M: Memory   KB-Kilobytes
             MB-Megabytes

The power of a PC computer depends on the type of processor, processor speed and memory

1950

1950 Mauchly and Eckert started the first company to sell computers to business.

1951 A computer, using 5000 vacuum tubes, was the first to store data on magnetic tape.

1952 The first hearing aids appeared on the market using transistors.

1953 A computer using thousands of tiny iron rings that could be magnetised and used to store data was introduced.

1954 The first silicon transistor was developed.

1955 Bill Gates, founder of Microsoft was born in Seattle, Washington. The first computer was built using transistors instead of vacuum tubes.

1956 The first hard disk was used to store data (5 megabytes).

1957 Plans were discovered in early correspondence for the first mechanical calculator, dating back to 1623.

1958 Thomas Watson, the founder of IBM (International Business Machines), forecast that there was a world need for only five computers! The integrated circuit was developed, the basis of all modern computers.

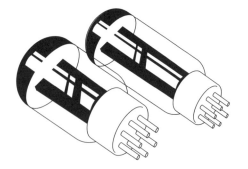

1959 The programming language COBOL, which is used for writing business programs, was invented.

1960 A computer was developed that, for the first time, used a keyboard and monitor.

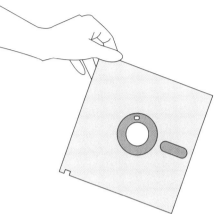

1961 IBM constructed a computer using over 169,000 transistors.

1962 The first robots used on the assembly line of an American car manufacturer.

1963 Police – the first computer used by the Metropolitan Police for pay and crime statistics.

1964 IBM developed the first Computer Aided Design (CAD) system.

1965 The first low cost ($18,000) computer with 4 kilobytes of memory sold.

1966 Computer data transmitted for the first time on light beams in strands of glass (fibre optic cables).

1967 The idea of a computer network first proposed.

1968 The first computers to be built using integrated circuits instead of transistors and the first computer mouse demonstrated.

1969 On 1 October two computers were networked together for the first time. Birth of the Internet with four computers linked to the network by the end of the year. Banks – the first cash machines (ATMs) were installed in the United States (not networked).

1970   Computer storage – the floppy disk and a 1 kilobyte (1 KB) memory chip – is seen for the first time.

1971   The first pocket calculator, weighing more than 1 kg, produced by Texas Instruments.

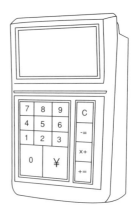

1972   Email was developed and used for the first time.

1973   10,000 components were placed onto a computer chip 1 cm^2.

1974   The Police National Computer came online. The *Radio Electronics* magazine described how to build a personal computer. Laser scanners and bar codes introduced in some US supermarkets.

1975   The first word processor software was developed. IBM developed the first laser printer. Tesco stores started trials in UK using EPOS (Electronic Point of Sale) terminals at the checkout and scanning bar codes.

1976   The first supercomputer was built, the CRAY-1.

1977   Ken Olson, the president of DEC, declared there was no reason for anyone to have a computer in their home! Bill Gates started the company Microsoft.

1978   Personal computers used floppy disk drives for the first time.

1979   Japan trialled the first network of mobile phones. Britain introduced its first computerised telephone exchange. The first spreadsheet program was developed for microcomputers.

1980

1980   The first database program was produced for personal computers.

1981   In New York, IBM launched its smallest, lowest-priced computer, the IBM PC.

1982   Disney released *Tron*, one of the first movies to use computer-generated graphics. Compact disc players were introduced and the first CD produced was the album *52nd Street* by Billy Joel.

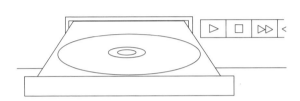

1983   The US Department of Defence adopted the network standard for the Internet. The first computer virus was produced as a research project. Hard disk drives developed for the personal computer.

1984   Apple produced the Macintosh computer with a graphical user interface. Hewlett Packard produced the first laser-jet printer, printing eight pages per minute with a resolution of 300 dpi.

1985   Intel developed the 80386 chip, running at 33 MHz and incorporating 275,000 transistors. Microsoft shipped the first version of Windows for the PC.

1986   Amstrad launched the very successful PC1512 – at only £399 it captured 25% of the European market within six months.

1987   The 3.5" floppy disk became the standard over the earlier 5.25" disk.

1988   Microsoft became the top selling software company and the millionth Microsoft mouse was sold. The first fibre optic cable was laid across the Atlantic ocean capable of carrying over 37 000 telephone conversations.

1989   Intel developed the 80486 chip running at 50 MHz and incorporating 1.2 m transistors.

1990

1990   Microsoft launched Windows 3.0 that supported large graphical applications.

1991   Hewlett Packard launched the first palmtop device weighing only 11 ounces.

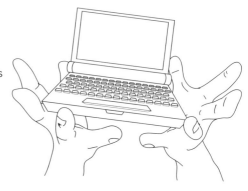

1992   Digital mobile phones were introduced in the US.

1993   Intel launched the Pentium processor running at 66 MHz and incorporating 3.1 million transistors.

1994   The Internet 'Yahoo!' was launched with its directory of Web sites and topic categories.

1995   Microsoft launched Windows 95 (over one million copies sold in the first four days). Tesco supermarkets launched loyalty cards for customers.

1996   Metropolitan Police launched their Web site. Microsoft launched 'Hotmail', its free email Internet service.

1997   The first trials of the National Automated Fingerprint Identification System (NAFIS). The IBM computer 'Deep Blue' defeated the reigning World Chess Champion, Gary Kasparov.

1998   Microsoft became the biggest company in the world, valued at $261 bn.

1999   Plastic cards were issued by banks with integrated circuit chips for better security. 275 million mobile phones and 30 million laptop computers sold worldwide.

2000

2000   Microsoft launched Windows 2000. The number of Internet users in the UK rose above ten million. Small and medium-sized businesses using the Internet reached 1.7 million. Hotmail, Microsoft's free email service, had 66 million active users.

2001   Fingerprint Identification System due to be used by all 43 police forces.

2002   Forecast introduction of 3G (third generation) mobile communications with data speeds of up to 2 Gbps.

2003   Forecast 2.4 million workers in the UK, 10% of the workforce, will be working from home.

2004   Estimated $1,400,000,000,000 (£960,000,000,000) of Internet business will take place worldwide.

2005   A UK government department report states that by 2005, everyone in Britain should have access to the Internet.

Answers

Computer software (page 11)

1 a The database, Microsoft® Access, could be used by the hotel to record the charges incurred by the guests. One of the tables in the database would hold records for all the guests of purchases made with fields for room number, location and amount spent. When the guest checks out of the hotel, a database search is made using the room number and each record found is printed out as a report. Access reports include the facility to total columns of numbers, in this situation, the report would show the total spent.

  b Three from the following: Word processing – letters sent by the hotel to guests, suppliers, maintenance contractors, etc; Desktop publishing – restaurant menus, notices, leaflets for excursions around the island; Spreadsheet – hotel accounts including modelling income and expenditure for hotel and sailing activities; Internet – monitor weather conditions, hurricanes and tropical storms and provide daily forecasts for the sailing instructors and guests. Monitor exchange rates for US$, EC$ (Eastern Caribbean) and £sterling; Email – supply ordering and message services for guests and staff.

2 Microsoft® PowerPoint presentation software.

3 Words in correct order are: outsourcing, software, rented, ASP, Hotmail.

4

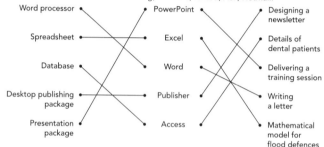

The Internet (page 30)

1 Words in correct order are: quickly, spelling, search, encryption.

2 Features may include: Web pages poorly designed and difficult to navigate; pages with spelling and grammatical errors; difficult-to-find products; order pages too complicated and time-consuming to use; poor security for credit card details and numbers; poor and slow responses to customer enquiries; customers not informed that goods out of stock, late deliveries.

3 Ideally, each of the pages should have a two-way link with every other page. In the illustration shown, users moving to the help page from the products page would be unable to return. Also, there is no way to return to the home page.

4 a B2B – Business to Business (sites created by businesses for use with other business).
  b B2C – Business to Consumer (sites created by businesses to advertise and sell to customers).

5 Web site – need for site in different languages, products priced in different currencies. Business – include cost of delivery, consider different countries' regulations to health and safety with electric toys, method of providing customer service and the warranty of models, etc.

6 It increases the network traffic and slows down the performance for genuine business activity. Employees waste work time in reading, sorting and deleting the spam emails from their mail boxes. Both, clogging the network and losing employees time, costs business money.

7 3G mobile phones have an 'always on' connection to Internet (2G needs to dial up the connection when the Internet is required), 3G uses UMTS system transmitting data at 2 Mbps (2G uses GSM which only transmits data at 9.6 kbps).

ICT in supermarkets (page 40)

1 a Too much stock – takes up space and products may not be sold before their 'sell-by' date expires.
   b Too little stock – customers cannot buy goods and need to shop elsewhere.
2 Correct order: E, C, A, B, D
3 Customer A = 3, customer B = 1, customer C = 2.

ICT in banks (page 55)

1 a Making cards containing integrated circuits that are very difficult to copy.
   b It will take several years to change the cash machines (ATMs) and upgrade the electronic tills (EPOS terminals) in shops.
2 Words in correct order are: credit, clearing, banks.
3 ATM – Automatic Teller Machine, PIN – Personal Identification Number, EFTPOS – Electronic Funds Transfer Point Of Sale, ICC – Integrated Chip Card, MICR – Magnetic Ink Character Recognition, BACS – Bankers' Automated Clearing Service.
4

ICT in the police (page 63)

1 NAFIS – National Automatic Fingerprint Identification System, CRIS – Crime Reporting Information System, PNC – Police National Computer, GRASP – Global Retrieval, Access and information System for Property, HOLMES – Home Office Large Major Enquiry System, PHOENIX – Police and Home Office Extended Names IndeX.
2 Hendon, London.
3 Vehicle database with 48 million records (criminal database – approximately 5 million records).
4 Words in correct order are: million, eight, compare, second, criminal.
5 a Michael Hunter.
   b Noel Ellis.
   c Joe Hooper.
   d Nicholas Wetton.
   e Carl Robinson has green eyes and is driving a modern car – the reg letter for Carl is X (2000), the other car belonging to a man with green eyes has a registration letter dating the car to 1966/67.
   f James Troy is the only suspect whose car registration could be personalised to his name, ie JAT.

ICT in the car industry (page 73)

1 a Electric motors – very precise positioning required.
   b Hydraulic systems – very strong and can handle heavy weights.
   c Pneumatics systems – allow rapid movement of the welding arm.
2 The price of robots is at an all time low, or the requirement for flexibility in manufacturing is increasing or the health and safety implications of many tasks make manual operation undesirable.
3 Words in correct order are: aided, drawings, two-dimensional, data, manufacture.
4 First generation robots were not equipped with sensors to provide feedback to the controlling computer. Second generation robots were closed loop systems providing feedback that enabled the control software to alter the robots actions.

113

ICT in the health service (page 80)

1 Information in the records more structured; Can access records from remote locations; Can search and retrieve information very quickly; Records take up less space; Easy to keep backup copies of the data; Can search records and gather statistical information for research; Computer can cross-reference new prescriptions with existing medication to check for possible dangers; Medical data can be kept more secure with password protection; Possible to allow different levels of access to the data depending on the person, ie administration staff have limited access.

2 Words in correct order are: tomography, three-dimensional, organs, detect.

3

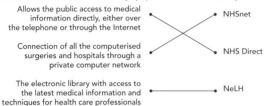

Allows the public access to medical information directly, either over the telephone or through the Internet	→ NHSnet
Connection of all the computerised surgeries and hospitals through a private computer network	→ NHS Direct
The electronic library with access to the latest medical information and techniques for health care professionals	→ NeLH

4 It would be necessary to input data to identify the patient, otherwise they would only know how many meals of each kind were needed but not where to deliver them. The patient would usually be identified by a unique number. The hospital ward number may also be read from the form.

5 a

Upper limit	2.6	2.6	3.2	2.7	3.2	5.2	8.1	2.1	2.6	3.1	3.9	3.5	2.7	2.6	2.5
Incoming data	2.5	2.5	3.0	2.6	3.0	5.1	8.0	2.0	2.5	3.0	3.8	3.6	2.6	2.5	2.4
Lower limit	2.3	2.3	2.8	2.5	2.8	5.0	7.9	1.9	2.4	2.9	3.7	3.3	2.5	2.3	2.2

b   alarm triggered

c   iii If 'data value' < 'lower limit' OR 'data value' > 'upper limit' then trigger alarm.

ICT in home working (page 85)

1 Words in correct order are: home, stress, greater, people, isolated.
2 a Three from: computer (desktop or laptop), printer, scanner, Webcam or digital camera, Internet connection.
   b Three from: improved quality of life; no travelling to office so less stress, no cost and time saved; flexible working hours, increased self-esteem, can look after children.
3 Two from: ADSL – asymmetric digital subscriber line; ISDN – integrated services digital network; broadband.

ICT in car inspections (page 89)

1 Words in correct order are: customers, head office's, vehicle, date, electronically.
2 a PDA – personal digital assistant.
   b Waterproof covering, hardwearing shell.
   c Portable printer and mobile phone.
3 Quarter of a million in the year gives an average of 683 per day (250,000/366 days). [Note that the year 2000 was a leap year.]
4 a One from: 'data entry' staff costs reduced, time and money saved by downloading appointments directly to engineer's computer, less paperwork.
   b One from: printed report for customer directly after inspection, less chance of data errors, more flexible appointment system, enhanced checklists possible for individual models of vehicles.

ICT in call centres (page 92)

Words in correct order are: help, integrated, information, track, FAQs.

ICT in air traffic control (page 96)

1   Two from London: Heathrow, Gatwick, City, Stansted, Luton. Others include: Birmingham, Manchester, East Midlands, Liverpool, Leeds, Newcastle, Glasgow.
2   NATS – National Air Traffic Services Ltd, ATC – air traffic control, FDPS – Flight Data Processing System, RADNET – RAdar Data Distribution Network, ASTERIX – All purpose STructured Eurocontrol Radar Information eXchange.
3   Words in correct order are: NATS, Swanwick, S/390, flight, maintenance, communication.
4   a

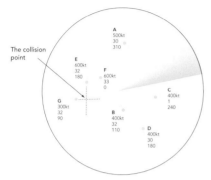

b   Aircraft C is flying at only 1000 feet which is too low for normal air traffic. Instructions from the controller to the pilot would be to climb to a safe altitude.

ICT in weather forecasting (page 103)

1   Land-based stations, weather balloons (radiosonde), satellites, radar, aircraft, ships, buoys.
2   Words in correct order are: computer, Met, five, Cray, gigaflops, operations.
3   a   Temperature, wind speed, wind direction, air pressure, humidity.
    b   By a radio link or cables connections.
4

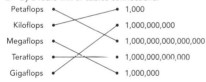

Internet reference sources

The following Web addresses were correct at the time of going to print. However, due to the nature of the Internet some may have moved or no longer exist.

Voice over IP

- Technology for long-distance calls on the Internet – www.callserve.com/EN

Application Service Providers

- The list of ASPs – www.asp.thelist.com
- ASP Industry Consortium – www.aspindustry.org
- ASP explanation on the excellent How Stuff Works site – www.howstuffworks.com/asp1.htm

Mobile phones

- Mobile Internet – www.ericsson.com
- Software systems – www.symbian.com
- General WAP information – www.wapforum.org
- Wireless data applications – www.mobileways.de

Banks

- Bank of England – www.bankofengland.co.uk
- Bankers' Automatic Clearing Service (BACS) – www.bacs.co.uk
- Association for Payment Clearing Services – www.apacs.org.uk

Police

- PITO – www.pito.org.uk
- History of fingerprints – www.met.police.uk/history/fingerprints.htm
- Information on NAFIS (fingerprint identification) – www.pito.org.uk/our/products/nafis/profile.asp

National Health Service

- NHS Direct – www.nhsdirect.nhs.uk
- NHS Information Authority – www.nhsia.nhs.uk
- National electronic Library for Health – www.nelh.nhs.uk

Air Traffic Control

- National Air Traffic Services – www.nats.co.uk
- Civil Aviation Authority – www.caa.co.uk

Weather Forecasting

- Met Office – www.met-office.gov.uk

ADSL – (Asymmetric Digital Subscriber Line). This is a method of communicating across a wide area network such as the Internet. The data, which passes along existing copper telephone lines, travels at different speeds depending on the direction. From the Internet to the home or office, data travels at speeds of up to 8 Mbps (eight million bits per second). In the opposite direction, from the computer back to the Internet, data travels at speeds of up to 640 Kbps (640 thousand bits per second).

Algorithm – An algorithm is a sequence of steps or instructions designed to solve a task or problem. Computer programmers design algorithms to solve problems and carry out tasks such as sorting and searching data.

Bandwidth – Bandwidth is used to describe the quantity of data that can travel along a data channel. For example, a copper wire, fibre optic cable, wireless or satellite link. Data flow, which is measured in bits per second (bps), is greater for channels with wider bandwidths.

Binary Digit (Bit) – Data in a computer is made up of binary digits (ones and zeros). Each letter on the keyboard is coded by eight binary digits, for example, the letter A is represented by the computer as '01000001'.

Broadband – Broadband describes a communication channel that has a wide bandwidth and can carry a large quantity of data. Over the years broadband has been defined by giving it a numerical value, for example 34 Mbps (34 million bits per second) of data. With numerical value, however, has changed as the technology has improved. Under a recent government scheme, broadband connections are being installed in many UK schools to improve the speed of Internet connections.

HTML (Hypertext markup language) – The computer language which is used to organise and publish Web pages.

Internet server – A computer that makes information available to the network.

ISDN (Integrated Services Digital Network) – This is a method of communicating across a wide area network such as the Internet. The data, which can use existing copper telephone lines, travels at speeds of 64 Kbps (64 thousand bits per second). Often, two channels are used along the same wire, one for incoming data and one for outgoing data. The use of two channels increases the speed to 128 Kbps. Many schools used ISDN connections for their Internet before moving to broadband connections.

Leased line – This is a dedicated line that is installed for communication between two points. Because the line is not shared with other users it provides a reliable and fast channel for data communications and there is no need to dial as the number is always connected. Businesses use leased lines between their offices and between major suppliers and customers.

Mainframe – Mainframe computers are used in large companies for data processing and by scientists for complex mathematical calculations. They are also used as network servers on the Internet. On average, a mainframe would cost about £4 m and an example of a mainframe is IBM's System/390.

MPEG-3 (MP3) – An audio compression system which enables CD-quality sound to be compressed by a factor of about 12 without a noticeable loss of quality (from approximately 1.4 Mbps to approximately 120 Kbps). Higher compression ratios can be achieved, but only by sacrificing quality. Because MP3 files are small, they are readily transferred across the Internet, which raises many copyright concerns.

TCP/IP (Transmission Control Protocol/Internet Protocol) – TCP/IP has become quite a common term used by people involved on the technical side of using the Internet. The word 'protocol' means an 'agreed standard', and so this expression concerns the set of standards used to ensure that different networks, for example local area networks and wide area networks will work when connected together.

Windows NT – This is a version of the Microsoft® Windows operating system designed for networks. The program provides a user-friendly screen with windows, icons and menus which enables the user to manage the network. The operating system, which is a very complex program, can handle many users (multi-user) and many tasks (multi-tasking) at the same time.

Unix – This is an operating system written in the programming language C. It is a multi-user, multi-tasking operating system often found on larger systems like minicomputers and mainframes but it can also be used on microcomputers.

Video conferencing – Refers to users communicating across networks using audio and video images. It is ideal for meetings between remote sites or different countries around the world. A camera, often placed on the top of the monitor, records the digital images of the user while a microphone captures the speech. These signals are then transmitted across the network to the receiving station where the image is displayed in a window on the monitor. Data from applications can also be transmitted, eg graphs, spreadsheets, etc.

Index

Qq

Rr

Ss

Tt

Uu

Vv

Ww